My Journey To
Freedom

2nd Edition

G. R. GOLDING

Kingdom Publishers

My Journey to Freedom
Copyright© G. R. Golding

All rights reserved. No part of this book may be reproduced in any form by photocopying or any electronic or mechanical means, including information storage or retrieval systems, without permission in writing from both the copyright owner and the publisher of the book. The right of G.R. Golding to be identified as the author of this work has been asserted by him/her in accordance with the Copyright, Designs and Patents Act 1988 and any subsequent amendments thereto.
A catalogue record for this book is available from the British Library.

ISBN: 978-1-913247-18-8

2nd Edition by Kingdom Publishers
Kingdom Publishers
London, UK.

You can purchase copies of this book from any leading bookstore or email
contact@kingdompublishers.co.uk

Introduction

I always feel relief after transferring my worries and concerns that are spinning around in my head to paper. In fact, at night, when things trouble us the most, I sleep with a pen and paper by my bed! I know that once I have written down any concerns that are keeping me awake, they are out of my head and I can settle to sleep.

For many years I have hesitated to write my testimony. I have longed to get 'my journey' on to paper and to be relieved of it all. My hesitation has been the effect that it may have on those who do not know Jesus personally and who may find it hard to understand the struggles and difficulties that Christians sometimes go through. But it is through these times we can grow in our walk with Christ and learn through our search for the truth among the many misleading signposts and pitfalls that we may encounter during our lives.

Now that I have written these experiences down, I feel this great relief having put in order the things that happened and have it all exposed. I hope that it has been written in a way that will not damage the church or bring reproach on its people, but rather that others will see how God brings us through and helps us to rise above our circumstances causing us to worship and praise Him for the things He has taught us and shown us along the way.

To protect the identity of those who were involved, and who are not aware that I am writing my testimony I have changed their names.

Lastly, I want to take this opportunity to thank Joyce Stammers for editing this book. I can never thank her enough for her support and friendship, she has given to both my husband and I on this Journey *to Freedom*.

CONTENT

The Home	9
My Accident	17
Meeting God	23
Our Sister	26
Our Grandparents	31
Oakham	34
The Trauma	40
From Oakham to Morecambe	47
A Struggle Ended	56
New Ministry with Devastating Results	61
Our Five Children	68
Commands and Demands	77
Rules and Demands Increase	81
Separation and Excommunication	84
My Search for the Truth	97
Heart Brakes and Reunions	107
New Beginnings	111
Moving On	119
Epilogue	123

The Home

Hi there! let's begin with my very first memories and suggest that, if your name is Peggy, Beryl, Eunice, Rachel, Dennis, Oswald, Peter or Tom and you were brought up in a children's Home in Alma Road, Boscombe, Bournemouth, in the mid. 1930's; a Home run by a Mrs Palmer and her daughter who was known to us as Auntie Claire, then you may have remembered me a child by the name of Wendy, if so my story may interest you.

I was too young as a baby of 12 months to remember the day I joined you but I do remember so well, at the age of six waving goodbye to you all. In those years together we became a family and I still remember you all by name.

Peggy, you were older and did much of the house work. When I think of you, I see you in an apron with a brush in your hand standing at the foot of the stairs and daring me to go up them with my shoes on.

Oswald, you were older still. I remember you as someone to be afraid of, and no wonder, for I still see you now as I came down in the mornings, seeing you sitting at the kitchen table, demanding to know if I had wet my bed and how you threatened to put me in the copper if I had. That was the old copper that stood behind you and where all the washing was done, I really thought you meant it and one day you would be true to your word.

Beryl, Eunice, Tom, Rachel and Peter. We must all have been the same age; we always played together and ate together. Do you remember that long bench we would all sit along at meal time? Auntie Claire would spread the marge on the bread leaving the pattern of the serrated carving knife over the surface, and call it best butter.

My worst memories are of those of you chasing me around the house or garden with live spiders and the day you held me down and put a striped garden spider down my back. You have no idea what that did to me and the phobia it left me with even to this day but one thing it did teach me, was never to tell any other child that I had this fear in case of a re-occurrence of such an incident again.

Beryl, do you remember the day we started school together? We were both four years old and both holding hands with fear we would be split up and left with people we did not know. They let us sit together didn't they? But it wasn't long before we were confident enough to make our own friends and we were moved to different classes.

Do you remember the day we started using swear words we had picked up from school And how we got punished by Auntie Claire with mustard being pushed into our mouths and sent to bed? But instead of being remorseful or repentant, we kept repeating to each other as many bad words that we could think of.

Like most children we were no angels but I guess none of you ever knew until now that I was the one who paid the halfpenny each day for milk but always left it in the crate untouched and each day waited to hear the teacher say" Whose milk is this not drunk?" I would remain silent; too afraid to let anyone know that it was mine. You probably have forgotten it but it is one of my first deceitful memories. I didn't tell anyone but I knew milk often made me sick and I would be bringing it up again either in the play ground or in the toilets after drinking it. I knew too that Auntie Claire had put the fear of God into us on many occasions if we wasted food and wouldn't take kindly to wasting her money either.

Dennis, you were the oldest and must have been about fourteen when we started school. You had a tradesman's bike with a big metal carrier on the front. You would sit me in the carrier and peddle me to school. I remember you telling me I was your favourite, and you always made sure I was out of the way when you were teasing and pushing the other children around. Do you remember the beaded necklace you gave me? I'll tell you later what happened to that.

Auntie Claire's mother, Mrs Palmer, seemed very old to me. She suffered with swollen ankles and would get us children sitting at her feet rubbing her ankles trying to relieve the pain. Auntie Claire was very strict and no one wanted to displease her.

I don't remember my brother arriving at the Home or what age he was when he arrived. He was 16 months younger than I was. I had been told I was sent there when I was 12-months old. My earliest recollections were feeding him with little square pieces of bread through the bars of a playpen and later being responsible for dressing him. It seemed to me he would spend most of his days strapped in a high chair or in a playpen.

There are two incidents I vividly remember with my brother Reginald. One; the bottom sheet of his cot had been pinned down with safety pins to stop the sheet from roughing up, but he managed somehow to undo one of the pins; taking it out, putting it in his mouth and swallowing it. He was choking and vomiting so badly and no one knew what was causing it. Eventually he was taken to hospital where they discovered this open safety pin lodged in his throat and removed it.

The second incident was when he had pneumonia. Mrs Palmer woke me up one night to tell me the doctor had told them he would not last the night out. Of course, there were no antibiotics in those days; so many illnesses were much harder to cope with. I had been called to go and see him while he was still alive. At that point, I felt I had something to do with his illness and I had yet to realise that he was any more special to me than the rest of you in the home. I looked at him and remember thinking he was already dead. After what seemed ages I was sent back to bed where I cried quietly for some time in the darkness. There were four of us in the same room and woe betides us if we woke each other up. Why I thought was this child more important to me than all the others at the Home? I knew it was my job to feed him and dress him, in this place we were all brothers and sisters; why was I especially responsible for this one? No one told me we were related.

Well, God evidently had other things in mind because in the morning I was told he was still alive. Mrs Palmer had stayed up with him all night using her own remedies on him. Gradually he began to recover. It took a long time and he was three years old before he could walk again. Do you remember how we used to sit on that long bench and laugh at him trying to walk?

I remember the day war was declared. We came home from school to be told we were at war with Germany. I was four and it didn't seem all that important to me, but there was an excitement in the air and a lot of chatter among the older generation. Of course it meant more when the bombs started dropping. Portsmouth was bombed heavily which wasn't too far from Bournemouth and we had to learn that, when the high-pitched sound of the siren was heard, we all had to dive for cover.

There were two places in the house regarded as safer than any other. One was in the cupboard under the stairs, where you could fit about three of us children and one adult. An electric light was fixed in the cupboard and cushions kept there for us to sit on. The other place was under the large dining table with sheets placed over its top reaching down to the floor. The rest of us would crouch under it and, from there, we would often hear a bomb or two dropping somewhere.

Our bedrooms would be very dark at nights as we had to have blackout material at our windows so that the German planes could not see us. Do you remember the night Auntie Claire was drawing the curtains and instead of drawing them before she put the light on, as she should've done, she put the light on the first and then went to draw the curtains? As a result, she was shot at by a German plane; the shrapnel came through the window but fortunately it missed her. For this reason there were no streetlights on the streets at night and torches had to be shone towards the ground.

Remember those Mickey Mouse gas masks we carried to school on our shoulders and how we had to practice putting them on. I'm sure we would never have got them on in time if there had really been a gas alert and weren't they hot and stuffy?

Now I don't know why my brother and I were in this Home, I never got to ask. Somehow mother would never talk of her past. I do not know if it was because it was during the time of the slump in the 1930s and my father was out of work... or some other reason.

My brother and I were both born in Bournemouth. Our parents must have moved to London and living in a one bed flat. I can remember my father coming to see me once and taking me to the beach but I don't remember my mother ever coming, perhaps she was too busy. We had a special sitting room where parents and visitors went. We were never allowed to go in unless with visitors.

You know, I never missed my parents. I suppose it was because I did not really know them. We were never special to anyone but, to us, it seemed we were treated alright. We knew no other way of life.

After my father had taken me to the beach, he decided to take me home to his flat in London but as soon as we arrived I knew my mother was not happy. I heard her saying to my father: "What have you brought her here for?" Not too nice for a child to hear and I must admit I felt uncomfortable.

The very next morning my mother took me on a train, when I asked where I was going she said "The zoo". In fact, there was no zoo. I was being taken back to the Home. We got a taxi from the train back to the Home. The taxi waited for my mother to deliver me then drove off again. I don't remember feeling any emotion. I was back home where I belonged and with you who I had grown up with. There was no one there to say: "why have you brought her back?" I was just glad to be back where I belonged, although I was sorry there had been no zoo.

I was six and a half the day by mother turned up in a taxi again, and that was to take my brother and me to live with them. Father had now found a job which had caused them to move to Chester to a place called Little Sutton. They had found a council house to rent with three bedrooms and we were now going there to live as a family.

I can remember so well that day we said goodbye to you all and, Dennis that was when you gave me the necklace: a keepsake you said.

As I got into the taxi, I looked back to see you all waving outside the front of the house. I felt sadness and yet excited as to what was about to happen. Here was the beginning of a new experience. That was the last I ever saw or heard of you again, and you never knew how much I missed you all in those first few weeks.

Well the taxi took us to the station. We had to wait on the platform sometime before the train arrived my brother and I sat on a seat either side of my mother waiting for the train. By this time I was already feeling a little weepy and holding back the tears; I didn't want her to see me crying. She was really a stranger at this point. I remember the coat she had on. It had a very large fur collar and I remember burying my face into it and feeling comfort from it.

There had been no conversation between us in the taxi and it was not until we had got to the station that my mother asked me if I was all right. I didn't know how to answer her so said nothing and from then on I decided not to say anything anyway. She told me I was being silly and we wouldn't get very far if I didn't talk to her, but the more she said, the less I wanted to talk. I suppose this was partly because I was not too certain as to what was happening. The train arrived and again my brother and I sat either side of our mother in the carriage and I eventually fell asleep with my head buried in her fur collar. I did not wake up until we had to change trains to get to Chester. It was cold and dark and having been taken out of my hiding place (the fur collar) nothing seemed to be going well as I burst into tears and refused to walk to the next platform to change trains. No amount of coaxing would make me move so in desperation, I suppose, my mother had to drag me along to the next train, something I resented her for, for the rest of the journey. I didn't make it easy for her. In the next train, I didn't want her fur collar or even to sit next to her, so sat opposite wanting with all my heart to be taken back to the children's home. Not a very good start but I guess it was all my fault: all those mixed emotions were hard for a six-year-old girl.

It was late when we arrived at our new house and I was too sleepy to take anything in. I just noticed my father was not there. His new employment as a heating engineer, took him away from home at times.

I awoke the next morning to discover I was in a bedroom all of my own. This had never happened to me before; it seemed strange as there were always four of us sleeping in one room at the Home. I looked around the room. The sun was shining through the window and there was a dressing table in one corner and pink curtains at the window against pink wallpaper. Obviously the room had been prepared for the arrival of a little girl. My mother came in."This is your very own room", she said. I did not answer her but continued to look around the room still not wanting to converse with her.

My mother left me to go into my brother. I jumped out of bed and looked out of the window. Below was the garden with a grass lawn and at the bottom of the garden, a wired mesh pen with chickens in it. That was typical of mother; we got used to chickens, ducks and rabbits and the outdoor life, She was a country girl at heart and would get up at 6 a.m. during October to go mushrooming; other times it would be picking blackberries, elderberries, wild raspberries or rosehips, then there would be cowslips, bluebells and other wildflowers. There would be long walks in the country or woods, ice-skating on the frozen pond or sledging in the snow. Mother, as I said, loved the outdoor life.

After surveying the surrounds on the upper floor, I decided to dress in the clothes that had been neatly put out for me. I descended the stairs to a very small hall or so it seemed to me, then I entered the living room. It was an average sized room, quite cosy with a black leaded coal fire place with an oven on one side. I remember mother reared her newborn chicks in it. At night when the fire had gone out she would put the chicks in a cardboard box lined with a soft cloth and that would keep them warm overnight. There was no central heating in those days; we would get up on a cold winter morning, scraping the frost off the inside of the windows and there would be no heat until the fire had been lit and taken hold. The gas oven would be lit too and the door left open to warm the kitchen.

The kitchen was just off the living room where we ate all our meals. There was a bathroom that led off from the kitchen.

The house seemed very small compared to the large premises I had left and it seemed so quiet and empty; there was no hustle and bustle as there would have been where I had come from. I felt this empty feeling: lonely and uncertain. I went upstairs to look for my brother. My mother was dressing him. I stood by the door and when she spoke to me, I turned and went downstairs again.

It was a strange house, in a strange place, with a mother I hardly knew. I don't remember how many days and nights I would cry to come back to you all at the Home.

As result of this experience, I have such great sympathy for foster children that get shipped from one place to another with nothing stable. I felt bad enough but what must they feel.

As I settled down in my new home, my mother gradually became the most important person in my life. My father, well it didn't take long to love him, was so kind and gentle. I have the fondest memories of him playing with us, sitting on his knee when he told us stories. Most of these stories were taken from his own experiences. He had fought in the First World War having joined up for the Army when he was fifteen years old by telling the authorities he was nineteen.

It seemed so many youngsters around that age did the same, not having any idea what they would have to face. They would join up before their parents were aware of what they had done.

Father was the youngest of thirteen brothers and sisters but we never got to see any of them apart from one called Lewis and that was only for a very brief time. Two of his brothers had died, I understand, from tuberculosis as so many did in those days. Eventually my father contracted it while Mother was carrying me. There had been much concern as to whether he had passed it on to me. Fortunately Father got over it. Mother put it down to the fact that he ate pounds and pounds of cod liver oil and moult. Thus we were given it throughout our childhood.

As mentioned, my father, at the age of fifteen, fought in the First World War on the front line in the Battle of Mons. Have you heard of the Angel of Mons? My father was there and witnessed it. You'll find the account in the history books. He described the sighting as a long, very bright, vertical light in the sky and those on the battle field took it as a sign that they would win that battle. They did win it, but there was only three left in my father's regiment, he being one of them. He told me of the terrible conditions they were fighting under, sleeping in the trenches and death all around. The fact there were only three left in his regiment describes how terrifying it must have been. He had a shell go through the middle of his left hand in that battle, so was not fit to serve in the Second World War.

I learnt about the Russian and French Revolution from the stories he told and, as gruesome as they were, I found them very interesting; my father loved history.

Sad to say, father had a drink problem. I'm told he picked this up when he was in the Army when they would give the lads whiskey to drink before sending them out of the trenches, encouraging them to kill. There was many a time when he would be overcome and distressed at the number of men he had killed in the war. There was no such thing as counselling then and for a fifteen-year-old this must have been horrendous. Maybe his continuous drinking helped him to blot out the memories.

When Father came home drunk he was never violent. He was the opposite: he would spend money we couldn't afford on silly presents for mother and he would tell how much he loved her. Mother used to get angry with him and throw them back at him saying. "You're drunk Charles, you're drunk," and he would say: "I'm not, Mary, I'm not." I think we were more afraid of mum than of dad on these occasions. Some nights the police would pick him up and he'd be spending the night in a police cell while mother would be out looking for him.

Our time with dad was very short, five years in all, but that comes later.

We didn't see much of the war in Chester. You would only hear the reports over the radio and to us children there may not have been a war on for all the notice we took at that time. While you may still have been diving for cover under the table in Bournemouth, we were playing in the streets and fields.

Most of our games were centred round the war. As children we played nurses and soldiers, battle fields and firing with imaginary guns using the brick air raid shelters that had been constructed on the road just outside our house, as our headquarters and torture chamber. The punishment when the enemy was captured was to kiss the nurses. I don't know who suffered the most: the nurses or the enemy. Of course you hardly ever saw a car on the roads as there were very few about. Nearly all the men were at war and you had to be quite well off to afford a car, so the streets were quite empty and safe for us to play. We had a field at the bottom of our garden and a gate leading into it. This field used to be our battleground.

My Accident

It was now some months since I had left you all, and I had reached the age of seven and life was about to change for me again.

We as children had all been picnicking in this field at the back of our house when we ran out of drinking water and, as our house was the only one with a gate leading to our back garden, I was asked to go back with the bottle and fill it with water. I ran through the garden gate and refilled the bottle at our kitchen tap but when I went to return to the others with it, I saw that the cows had gathered around the gate and I didn't want to have to push my way through them so decided to get to the field from the road. This would take longer but was better than being trampled on by cows, I thought.

However, as I left my front gate, I noticed the paperboy delivering papers. We would often ask him if we could push some of his papers through the doors, so I ran across the road, the bottles still in my hand, to ask him if he would let me deliver some of his papers. In my hurry, I tripped on the curb, I felt no pain, but blood was pouring from my right arm, in fact it was not just pouring, it was squirting. As the bottle smashed, it had cut deep into my right arm. My arm was almost hanging off. I got up screaming, trying to hold my arm on. I had severed all the tendons, both the main nerves and the artery that runs between the bones.

I remembered auntie Claire would run cuts and bruises under the cold tap. In my panic I did just that. I ran to the bathroom and tried to hold my arm under the cold tap which always came out with force. Of course this only made things worse, and blood sprayed all over the bathroom ceiling. At this point there was no one around to help me or tell me what to do. Mother had been next door when she heard my screams and came out to see what I was screaming about and, they tell me, she passed out.

Fortunately, just across the road from my house there happened to be a doctor just leaving a patient's house. He'd heard my screams, came out to see and, unbeknown to me, had followed me into our house, He managed to grab a man's hanky which he used as a tourniquet at the top of my arm to try and stem the bleeding. He told me to try and move my fingers. I found they would not move He stayed with me until the ambulance came. I kept asking everyone if I was going to die. Mother had come round by now and kept assuring me that I wasn't going to die but I didn't believe her. I remember the crowd of children that was standing around the ambulance as they carried me in. My brother was left with a neighbour while mother came with me.

I was put on the ward with what seemed to me to be all old people; probably only in their 30s it was just that there were no children. I remember mother walked down the corridor with me as they wheeled me into the ward.

They didn't send me straight away to the operating theatre. It was not until some of the patients in the ward started screaming for a nurse that they decided to take me down straightaway. The hanky was still at the top of my arm and must have worked loose and there was blood all over the sheets and blankets.

I had lost so much blood that I was not aware of what was going on. I think I passed out before the nurses arrived then came to in a hazy kind of way as they were wheeling me out of the ward to the theatre. I asked my mother where they were taking me, she replied, "To the pictures." This was the second time she had not been truthful with me but I learned from that, that I should always tell my children the truth, explain things to them and tell them what they can expect to happen. If not, they have to face alone that which you didn't want to tell them in case they made a fuss.

I looked for the screen where the picture could be shown, all I saw was a big white frosted glass window and thought that must be where the picture will be seen. But when they put the cotton wool over my face, with the ether on it, I struggled like mad. "What are they doing to me? How can I see the film with this over my eyes?" Then I heard someone shout:"Hold her down!"

The thought of being held down was worse. Gradually I felt myself drifting off to sleep but the experience had left a long-term effect on me. For years after, I was afraid to go to sleep at nights. I would never tell anyone of my fear. I felt mother wouldn't understand, and I didn't feel I could trust her. She would tell me all sorts of things to avoid telling me the truth or speak of things she thought I would not understand. For instance, when I asked where I came from and how I got on this earth, she said, like lots of other mums, she found me under a gooseberry bush, I knew this was not true, so Mother never got to know my inner thoughts and fears and I never confided in her very often. Maybe it was those years we spent apart while I was growing up with you, who knows, or it may be that mother never opened up to us.

I suppose things were more difficult in those days. Sex was never talked about and people were not as open as they are today. As I found out later, Mother had a lot of baggage from the past she was carrying and she never wanted to open the door and let us in. Her past was a closed book as you'll see, and looking back now, I can understand. My heart goes out to her. She had a hard life and I'm just telling you how things were.

I remained in hospital for one month but the operation was not a success and I was left with no feeling or movement in my hand. The muscles became wasted and the main nerves never reconnected.

Six months later they operated again opening the arm from the wrist to the elbow trying to join the main nerves that had not been joined the first time but they had withered and could not be joined. I was left with a hand that I could not use.

So I had to learn to write with my left hand. Father bought me a glass slate with a picture under it. Trying to keep the pencil on the lines was frustrating.

When you're young you want to be the same as everyone else; you don't want to be different so you hide your disabilities as much as possible. I was always ashamed of my hand and did not want anyone to know about it. I hated games and occasions when you had to hold hands with a partner because then I couldn't hide it.

Going from using my right to left hand resulted in me starting to stutter. I had to go to speech therapy and talk with a pencil between my teeth; I found that hard. Other children would copy me and I found I was losing my self-confidence. But I was determined to do what everyone else did. So that when my arm was in plaster and bandages and others were learning to knit, I would take the knitting needles and wedge one of them between the bandages and put the wool over the needles with my left hand. It was a slow process but it worked, although all the knit stitches turned out as stocking stitch.

When I reached the junior school, my writing was good enough to sit with those who, because they had learnt to write well, could then read library books at the back of the class while the others had to continue to learn to write. My stuttering was also improving by then.

In later life, I was building brick walls, concreting, fitted kitchen cupboards, dressmaking, making curtains and furniture covers and learning that where there's a will, somehow, there's a way, although I have never been able to play any musical instrument apart from a guitar.

Not long after the accident my father's work took us to Formby. I can't remember much about that time; nothing significant happened. I remember the toilet was down the garden. It was a wooden seat with two places for people to sit on side-by-side; a very strange setup I thought. There were buckets that were emptied into carts each week and I can still smell the disinfectant that was put into the tubs. The toilet house was full of cobwebs and spiders. Not my favourite things.

I hated school there, one of the reasons was that they were much more advanced in their education and I didn't understand what most of the lessons were all about. I remember it was an all girls' school.

There was a little more of the war action going on here. There was a firing range among the pine trees that grew along the road going down to the beach and you could hear the guns going off nearly all day. On account of this, we could only go down to the beach at certain times. That's all I can remember about Formby, probably because we were only there about six months.

From there we moved again; this time to London, Trinity Road, Wandsworth. I was nine by this time and so much had already happened in those first three years after I left the home.

The house was almost opposite Wandsworth Common. It was a three-storey house that Sir Thomas Hardy, the writer, had once lived in. How do I know? His name and date were written on a plaque on the front wall of the house. It was not only a three-storey house but it had a cellar that became our play room and later on used for private dancing lessons, tap and ballet. Father was an entertainer before he met mother, singing and tap dancing on stage. He was quite musical too. Our dancing teacher, Mrs White, would come in twice a week to give us lessons although I had already been sent to lessons when we were in Chester.

So we had left the quiet little town of Formby and were now in the thick of the bombing raids on London.

We saw houses that were there one day and then rubble the next. Sirens were going off night and morning while we dived for cover. The walls of the underground stations were lined with bunk beds where people would sleep at night for safety. The house we were living in had an Anderson shelter in the garden. This was a shelter underground with a tin roof and turf on top. The interior contained four bunk beds. The walls were white washed breeze blocks. The adults could hardly stand up in it and you had to duck your head and shoulders to enter through the small wooden door.

Sometimes you would see the roads cordoned off where an unexploded bomb had dropped and now was waiting to be defused. Sometimes we would see what would be called *dogfights*, which were German and English planes trying to shoot each other down. We would watch these from our underground shelter or from the school yard at play time.

When the Germans started sending over the flying bombs or the *doodlebugs*, as they were called, we had to sleep in the underground shelters every night. You could hear them coming but as soon as the engine stopped you knew they were landing; then you'd hear the explosion. Somebody or something would have been hit and you'd never know, when the engine stopped, if it would be you.

At this time, all school lessons were in the brick built shelters in the play ground, whereas before we would only go to shelter when the sirens went off. Now the Germans could send so many more of these *doodlebugs* over as they didn't need planes or pilots to fly them. They would send more at night than in the day as they were not so easy to detect at night. Our soldiers on the home front would search the night skies with search lights and then shoot them down before they reached land.

By now, all the women that could, had to go to work; some in the factories and others on the land. Most men were on the front line, so the women were needed. Mother worked in a factory where they made petrol cans. She said the noise used to drive her mad.

Although my brother and I were only eight and nine, children still had to be left in the care of schools and day centres. School, during weekdays, would provide us with our tea and occupy us until parents came to pick us up at the end of the day when their work shift was finished. Centres would look after us at weekends too. Often at weekends and, unbeknown to Mother, instead of going to the Centre, we would go off to the underground station and we'd spend time there going up and down the escalators with one or two other children from school.

Later we found that if you brought a penny platform ticket, you could go anywhere in London that you liked providing you didn't come up on top again where you'd have to hand your penny ticket in. We would hop on one train to another going all over London. This was so much more fun than just going to the Centre. At least we were safer there than above ground.

Everything was rationed: food, clothes, furniture, sweets, petrol and so on. If a greengrocer had a delivery of oranges or bananas, the word would get around and there'd be a huge queue up the street to the door of the shop, but often they would be sold out before it was your turn to be served. I think babies got concentrated orange juice and other vitamins. I remember the packets of dried egg powder Mother used to make scrambled eggs with. She used it for baking too but that was not too often as sugar and margarine were on ration as well.

Well, so much for the war at the moment. I expect there are things I have forgotten; at nine you can't remember all that went on.

Meeting God

Now I want to tell you the first time I heard God speak to me. We had been living with Mother now for three years. I was still nine. Mother was never one to demonstrate her feelings. She was not the cuddly sort and I never really missed it, never having been used to it, Mother was very down-to-earth and practical with a no-nonsense approach. She worked hard and never had a lot of time to spend on us. Father was not often around as he would be away sometimes for a month at a time. He'd be home some weekends; then off again. That's how it had been ever since we had gone to live with them. We were better off than a lot of families who had their fathers away fighting in another country. It must have been really hard on those women bringing up their children and going out to work while at the same time worrying if their husbands would ever come back.

On the first day in my London school, the teacher put me next to a girl who had the same name as me, "Wendy" and from then on we became good friends. She told me her parents were missionaries. I got her to explain to me what a missionary really was and learned that it had something to do with God, so I was not all that interested. God had no appeal to me although at school assembly every morning prayers would be said pleading with God to help us win the war. Apart from that, God was far and distant and was one that only watched and punished: as Auntie Claire would tell us when we misbehaved.

When my new friend invited me to go with her to a Christian camp, I was quite excited until Mother said she could not afford to pay the money it would cost. Her parents then wrote to my mother to say there would be no cost and that they would like to take me with their daughter; so that's what happened.

It was a place called Edenbridge: in the country away from the bombing.

It was good to be with so many other children again and I was really enjoying the time. But one night, as I was getting into my bed, which was against the wall, I saw a huge brown spider with its long legs sprawled out on all sides of its body, clutching to the wall just above the side of my bed. I froze. I thought of the times I had been chased by you and that spider you had put down my back. I had always kept my fear of spiders secret in case I got the same treatment again. So on this occasion, I kept quiet but in doing so I would have to sleep alongside this creature. The last thing I wanted was the girls chasing me around the room with it

We had been talking that evening about the love of Jesus and I had come away thinking to myself: "I don't suppose that love was meant for me because I was no one special." We were never brought up in the kind of environment that makes you feel special. In the Home we had been one of a number; looked after but never fussed over. Although things were better living with Mother, we were never made to feel that special. Father, when he was at home, would cuddle and play with us and I always looked forward to him coming home. For this reason I thought the love of Jesus was meant for others but not me. I don't think I was too worried about it just then, just took it as a matter of course.

But that night God showed me I was wrong. I prayed for the first time a prayer I have never forgotten. I was asking Jesus if I could be one of those He could love and would He please keep this spider on the wall exactly where it was until the morning I remember asking Him not to let it come near me or on my bed through the night. I said, "If you answer my prayer, and it is still there in the morning, then I will know that you love me too." I kept saying the same prayer over and over, until I fell asleep. I thought I would be all right if the spider didn't move. If it did, I had visions of it running all over me.

I was awakened in the morning by the girl next to me. "Wendy" she said, "Look at that big spider by your bed!" I nearly shot out of bed but then I remembered I had to keep my secret. The spider must have reacted to the excitement and I watched as it ran to the other end of the wall whereupon it was squashed by one of the other girls. Then I remembered my prayer. Jesus had answered it. He had kept the spider there all night and it had not moved. I felt a sudden excitement. He did love me after all! I was among those He loved! Some may say, "The creature may not have moved anyway," and you might be right, but I know God used that incident so I could see that I was included in His love.

The next morning was Sunday and we all marched off to church. As I sat there, I heard the preacher read from Revelation: "Lo, I stand at the door and knock." He said Jesus was standing at our heart's door and knocking for us to open it and let Him in.

"Jesus is knocking at your heart's door and He's waiting to come in and live with you. Won't you let Him in?" he said.

I responded, "Why shouldn't I let him come in if he loves me?" So there and then I asked Jesus in to my heart and I know he answered. I was on a high. I was full of excitement and had never felt like this before, I just wanted to stand up there and then and tell the whole world from the rooftops that Jesus had come into my heart. I couldn't wait to tell the major of the camp so, as soon as the service was over, I ran to tell her. All the others went back to camp but she took me for a walk while she told me more about the Lord Jesus. Everything she told me was thrilling to me. We sat down on the grass discussing my new found friend that loved me. Later we prayed together and I told her I wanted to be a missionary like Wendy's parents.

She just said, "Well, we will have to see: you are young yet, but God will have something for you to do."

When I arrived back from camp, I immediately told my mother I had let Jesus into my heart.

"Oh", she said, "I used to go to church once."

This interested me and I asked her which one.

"Not in London", she said, "but there is one like it in Streatham."

I begged her to take me.

"One day", she said and she left it at that.

Not long after that I joined the Girl's Life-Brigade which was held in the Methodist church just across the road from our house. Also, one evening a month, I would go to what was called *Christian Endeavour*. There we would meet with other youngsters to sing children's choruses or old Sankey hymns. Reginald used to join me for these occasions.

It was sometime later that Mother eventually got to take me to the kind of church she used to go to, but we will come to that later.

Our Sister

First I have to tell you of the day Mother and I were walking to the shops. It was on a Saturday morning and we had been silent for some time and were skipping along trying to avoid stepping on the joints in the pavement, as children do

Mother said, "Stop jumping about for a bit. I have something to tell you."

I did as she said and looked up at her.

She was silent again for some time, and then she said, "You have a sister."

"A sister?" I asked, "Where?"

Whatever was mother saying?

I had been living with her for three years and a sister had never been mentioned in all that time. Mother didn't seem to want to say much more or to enlarge on the subject just then; only that she was coming to live with us the following week. I could hardly believe it. I had a sister! Where did she come from? I learned later we did not have the same father, and this new sister was almost three years older than me. Her name was Barbara and I'll relate more of her history later.

My brother and I could not wait to meet her. Father was at home that Saturday and had gone to meet her off the train. We kept looking at the clock wondering how long they would be while, at the same time, closely watching any passengers who got off the buses that stopped just across the road. We could see the busses unloading their passengers from the upstairs window quite easily. I could see Mother was anxious as she had not seen Barbara since she was a baby and she was now twelve years old.

Then the bus we were waiting for arrived! We saw Father get off and now we strained our eyes to see the girl who was holding his hand. We rushed down the stairs shouting: "She's here, she's here!" We all stood in the hall to greet her. My brother and I in front with Mother behind. Here she was. Not a bit like us to look at. She was tall for her age, dark hair, big brown eyes, and rosy complexion and bigger boned than us. We had fair hair with smaller features and we had green or blue eyes. I often think her father must have been very handsome and she certainly must have looked like him because she did not look like Mother; well not until she got a lot older. I thought she was very good-looking and I was proved right when the boys started noticing her.

I learnt later that Barbara had spent the first three years of her life in a foster home and later, when money stopped coming for her keep, she was handed over to my mother's parents to look after.

We found she was really good fun to be with, but would get us all into all sorts of mischief. A real tomboy with a wild imagination. She would take us pinching apples out of neighbour's gardens. I remember once when we were caught and we had to drop the apples we had picked and run for it. Later on we thought of all those apples we had picked and left behind, so Barbara devised a plan to go back and get them. I was to dress up in our brother's clothes and he was to dress up in mine. Looking back there was not much sense in that but there you are... that is what she suggested and everything Barbara did and suggested, was tops. My brother was to put on my dress and straw bonnet and I put on his trousers and top. Of course, Barbara didn't come with us; that was not part of her plan. We didn't get as far as collecting the apples as my friend from school, Rita Upton, saw us in the distance and chased after my brother calling my name. He ran like mad so that she would not catch up with him. Needless to say, we never retrieved the apples, much to our Barbara's disappointment.

Barbara would tell us wild stories about her adventures and we believed every word she said (until we grew older and realized that some of her tails could not possibly have happened) She was someone to look up to and admire, although Mother never looked at all our misdoings the way we did.

Barbara and I would parade up and down Trinity Road in Mother's chiffon nighties, playing weddings while Mother was at work. Often we would get fed up with my brother and would lock him out of the house, making him climb up onto the second floor flat roof so he could climb in the bathroom window and get in. We would have a bit of peace and quiet in the time it took him to do this. I can remember us locking him out in just his underpants and vest on a cold day and he having to climb up in full view of anyone passing by. Of course, our play would be interrupted now and again by the sirens and we would have to dive for cover. We would not have got away with such behaviour in the children's home or by Mother if she had known.

Barbara did have a serious side to her at times. I learnt from her that Mother's parents, our grandparents, who we had not yet met, and our great-grandparents on grandpa's side, were all Christians and had been praying for us. I guess that my acceptance of Jesus Christ so early in my childhood had been the fruit of their prayers.

The Christians our grandparents met with were then a bible believing fellowship with a genuine desire to follow the scriptures. It was with these believers Mother had been brought up, but not a word was ever spoken to us about Christianity by her. Any Christian teaching I was getting was from the Girls Life Brigade and the Methodist Church. So I was most surprised to hear that Mother already knew about Jesus Christ and had said nothing apart from the fact that she used to go to church when she was younger. I thought growing up with these believers would have meant much more to her than just going to church.

Then Barbara began to tell me what her grandparents had told her about her father: Mother had met him when she was about eighteen while they were both working in the same Gentry's house. I think Mother was employed there as a parlour maid but I don't know in what position Barbara's father had been employed. I only know that, as a result of their relationship, Barbara had been born. Consequently, Mother came under assembly discipline and was subsequently excommunicated from the Fellowship. It was at this point she left home; leaving Barbara in the hands of foster parents. Now I understood the reason for Mother's silence on these matters.

Poor Mother, she never got over the stigma of all that and it was considered to be much more shameful in those days than how the world regards such things today. I can fully understand why she never wanted to speak about her past. So many others have submitted to temptation but have never been found out. Mother carried the shame all her life.

Barbara went on to tell me that her father's parents lived in Ireland and that he had intended to marry Mother in spite of both sets of parents being against it. On a return trip from Ireland, after visiting his parents, the boat Mother thought him to be on, sank. Mother was never sure if he had got on that boat but she never heard any more from him so assumed he must have been on it and drowned.

Between the two world wars, my father had spent fifteen years in the Navy as a chef, when my mother met him they were both working in Lyons Corner house: a chain of eating houses which were very well known throughout the country. It wasn't many weeks after meeting that they were married.

When the 1930s economic slump arrived, as I have already mentioned, Father was out of work and it was left to Mother to bring home the money. Women didn't get paid the same wage as a man would in the same job so it must have been hard for them. With no financial help from the government, it must have been very difficult. I was born two months premature and Mother's teeth crumbled away after she gave birth to my brother as a result of her poor diet and lack of calcium. My brother lost all his teeth at nineteen.

Well after my experience at the Christian camp and finding that my mother used to go to a church, I kept pressing her to take me to the kind of church she used to go to but she always found some excuse not to do so, until I became ill with jaundice and had to remain in bed for three weeks. It was then she promised that, when I got better, she would take me to the kind of church she was bought up in. It was at a church gathering in Streatham that I remember my first encounter; all the ladies wore hats and the men smart suits. They were very friendly and made us feel welcomed, although I didn't understand a word of what the preacher was saying but I did like the atmosphere there. After the service Mother and I were asked back for tea with a lady called Mrs Botral. As a result, and over a period of time, Mother started attending the church regularly, eventually making a commitment and returning to her Christian life among this fellowship which entailed stopping all our so-called worldly activities. No more dancing lessons, no more cinemas, no radios, and so on. My father seemed to go along with all Mother's commands at the time and, as far as I know, although he never became a member of this church and he never made it known if he was a Christian or not.

Back to the war. Things were getting worse and there were times when we would spend days and nights in the shelters and now Barbara had come to join us. The weekend that Father came home there would not be enough room for us all in the garden shelter, so she and I had to sleep in the underground shelter on Wandsworth Common, which would sleep about forty people. The shelter was shaped like a long corridor with bunk beds fitted along the walls with an electric fire both ends. If you were a regular night sleeper down there, you would keep the same bed with your bed left made up and that would be regarded as your own bed. The spare beds were the ones that were not made up for people like us that were not regular occupants. We would have to take our sheets, blankets and pillows down there each time. Men and women were mixed; with no embarrassments sometimes they would be singing what I called *war songs* such as: *We'll meet again, Pack up your troubles in your old kit bag* and other such songs, just to keep their spirits up.

I quite enjoyed it down in the shelter. There seem to be so much more going on than in the shelter in our garden. Together, the grownups would count the doodlebugs going off and would make guesses as where they thought each one had dropped. They would even tease each other as to whose house the "bugs" were landing on. One night we counted fifteen, one after another. We didn't know what would meet us when we emerged the next morning. One doodlebug had fallen on Wandsworth Common; not a lot of damage from the blast apart from some broken glass from blown out windows and blown over fences and brick walls.

Back in the shelter at home, Mother said Father was looking out of the shelter door and, each time he heard a doodlebug coming and the engine stop, he would pull the door closed with a piece of string wrapped round his finger (as if that would have saved them) and say, "Duck Mary! This one is ours."

When we children were alone in the garden shelter, we used to sing this little chorus:

Safe in the arms of Jesus
Safe on his gentle breast
Safe with his arms around us
Safe in his love we rest

This would make us feel safe, knowing Jesus would be looking after us. What happened next proved that this was indeed so.

Mother used to go to a certain cafe for her lunch every day, but on this particular day, she thought she would have a change and decided to go to another café. On her way back to work, she had to pass the café she normally went to, and found it had been hit by a bomb. The death and devastation she saw at that scene upset her so much that she came down to the school and called us out of the air raid shelter where we were having lessons. She took us straight home, packed our cases and then travelled with us on the train that same day to our grandparents.

Remember, we had never met our grandparents before. They were never mentioned or talked about to us by Mother. It was not until Barbara came to live with us that we knew we had grandparents. We knew my father's parents had died. Up until this moment, Mother had not seen them or corresponded with them since the day she had left home some sixteen years earlier. This was the beginning of another new phase in our lives; another step into the unknown.

Our Grandparents

Mother must have sent a telegram to them to say we were coming as Grandpa was waiting on the station to greet us. There were one or two people standing on the platform waiting for the train as it slowed down at this quiet little platform in Oakham. Oakham was just a small village in those days where everyone knew everyone.

As Mother was lifting down our cases, I noticed an elderly gentleman standing and searching the train and its passengers. I don't think any of us knew he would be there to meet us, at least we three children were not told, so I was not expecting to see anyone I knew and this old gentleman standing there meant nothing to me until Barbara, having recognised him, shouted from the carriage door: "Grandpa!" He wore an old trilby hat and under its brim I could see large bushy eyebrows. He took his hat off to greet us and I noticed a head of white curly hair and a well trimmed moustache. He was average height, but his posture seemed a little bent.

I can't remember any greetings, only Grandpa taking the cases off Mother. Maybe there were but it is difficult to remember everything; by then I was ten years old.

Grandpa walked us to his little cottage. Grandma was there to meet us. She had very soft fine hair that had not yet turned completely grey: not bad looking for an old lady, I thought. Grandma was French, and had lived in France until she married my grandfather. Having come from a well-to-do family, she was employed as a ladies maid making fine dresses for her employer and mixing with the aristocrats in the upper circle. She met my grandpa when she came over to England with her employer. He was the son of a farmer working on his father's farm, but Grandma fell in love with him and him with her.

I was told that Grandma found it very difficult after they were married to adjust to Grandpa's way of life as a farmer and she always remained *The Lady with a French accent*. She owned several properties in Jersey but they were taken over by the Germans when they occupied the island during the war. Sadly, as they retreated, they did as much damage as they could before they left and her property was left needing a great deal of money spent on repairs, which by then Grandma could not afford.

Our grandparents' little cottage was very cosy but was really too small for five extra people. The kitchen was only the size of a front porch with only enough room for a small table at the side of the cooker. This was where the washing up was done from a small enamel bowl. There was no sink or drainage. In fact, there was no water in the house at all. Wastewater was emptied down the drain in the yard. Four houses shared one water pump that stood in the middle of the yard where water came from an underground spring and was obtained by a hand worked pump. There was no inside toilet, and the one they had outside had to be flushed with a bucket of water drawn from the pump in the yard.

Leading off from this tiny kitchen, if that is what you could call it, was a small living room. A large table in the middle took up most of the room. A couch stood against one wall and was near enough to the table to be used as seats when we sat down for a meal. On the wall opposite was the old black leaded grate with an oven on one side of the fireplace. On the other side was a small boiler you would fill with water every morning for hot water during the day. Against the other wall was an old organ with stops and bellows you had to pedal up and down before you could get a sound out of it and above that was an old chiming clock with its pendulum swinging from side to side.

Off the living room was a small front room that looked onto the street. Grandma lived and slept in this room and would maybe come out about once a day. There was no electricity in the house; we had gas lamps with mantles that would give more light than a naked flame. Upstairs were three bedrooms with no light at all so we had to take candles to bed.

We had only expected to stay there for safety until the war was over so most of our belongings were still back in London, but just two days after arriving in Oakham; we heard that our home in London had been destroyed by a doodlebug.

That was the second time in one week Mother had been saved. God had a reason, I guess. We would have all been killed if Mother had not taken us away on that Friday afternoon because the bomb that destroyed our house fell the night after we left. Father was called from where he had been working and both he and Mother had to go on the Monday to look at what remained of the house and see what could be salvaged.

I could not sleep that night. I could hear the church clock chiming every half hour and I remember praying most of the night that they would come back again. Our house had been hit. How did I know they would come back alive? I don't think I had realised the danger we had been in while we were living in London; not until this happened. I could not rest until they were back safely.

On their return, they told us there was nothing to be salvaged from the house. Everything had been destroyed. Dennis, that is how I lost the necklace you gave me. I had kept it with me all that time. We were told our cat we had, had gone and we never knew if she had been killed or had just run away. You would often see animals wandering around bomb sites, probably looking for their owners or houses. Father told us the air raid shelter we had slept in so many times was flattened and we would no doubt have been buried alive.

Oakham

So with no home to go back to we all had to live with our grandparents in this tiny house.

Oakham as I said was only a small town, there was only one infant school, one junior school, and one senior school, plus a grammar school. Conrad and I were sent to the Church of England junior school as it was called. I hated it and with good reason.

There were a good number of children sent from London to Oakham as refugees and the headmaster of the school classed my brother and me as such even though we had lost our home and had no other home to go to but our grandparents.

The headmaster who I am not afraid to name and shame was called Mr Biggs, and our nick name for him was "Piggy Biggs." He had no time for these *foreigners* from London.

He had a reputation in the area of getting more pupils through the 11+ exam, as it was called then, with marks good enough to get them through to the grammar school than any other school in the area, but those of us who attended the school knew how he did it. He would take about 18 of the brightest pupils and concentrate on their teaching, while the rest of his class was sent into the spare classroom to read books, do sketches and play games with another teacher. All the *refugees* would be sent into this class. We would start the day off with the headmaster and have some lessons together and then we had to pack up our things to leave his class while he taught the others.

I remember he came into our class one day to give us a maths test. There were ten sums and he told us that, for each sum we got wrong, he would give us the cane. Fortunately I only had the cane the once but the girl next to me a *refugee* from

London named Molly, got nine out of the ten wrong and was administered the cane nine times on the same hand. We watched the blood rising to the surface of her palm; the cane had always to be on the left hand so it did not hinder our writing. I felt so sorry for her. Some of these *refugees* had such a hard time and she was one of them. I know, because I used to play with a girl named Jill with whom Molly was living. It was obvious that Molly was not wanted there and they treated her really rough.

You know ten and eleven is very young to be taken away from your parents, and then to be treated so unkindly. Some were treated really well but there were a few who were unlucky. Quite often you would see Molly sobbing as she did that day.

It was very quiet in Oakham, there were no bombs dropping here, even though there were two American aerodromes quite nearby; one at Loughborough and one at Cottesmore.

We would see the Americans in the park with the local girls, while us younger ones would have sweets and chewing gum thrown at us from their passing jeeps. Whenever we saw them in the street or park, we would go up to them and say: "Have you any gum chum?" They always seem to have plenty of everything while we were on ration books.

We also had the German and Italian prisoners of war working on the land. Italians wore brown uniforms and the Germans green. I used to feel sorry for them/ away from their families, although I know they were given a much easier time in our country than our lads were having in theirs. They were free to roam around the shops and town. Two of my friends at school were farmer's daughters and I would be invited on to their farms where you could see these prisoners working. They would often tease us and we them. I remember one of my friends putting a frog down the back of one Italian. He couldn't get his top off quick enough but he took it in good humour.

Do you remember the day war ended and the Germans surrendered? I wondered where you were then. Were you still at the children's home? Because I thought of you all that day and wondered if you were all celebrating as we were: street parties, banner waving, and fireworks. It was a wonderful time for everyone except, of course, those who had lost their loved ones: sons and fathers who never came back when the other armed forces were demobbed. We met quite a few widows and fatherless.

Rationing still continued for some time after the war as there was a great shortage of everything Industry still boomed for several years after the war because there were so many things we had, had to do without because the factories had been turning out instruments of war instead of household needs for over five years.

Grandpa had a small cottage he had been renting out. The tenants had now left so Grandpa said we could have the cottage rent-free. By then we had been living with our grandparents for around eighteen months. It had been very difficult living in such cramp conditions but we were thankful to have had shelter and safety during that time. Now we were going to have a place of our own again.

The cottage needed a lot doing to it before we could move in. Mother put us children to scraping the wallpaper off the walls, which were about four layers thick. We were trying to get it ready for Father to wallpaper when he came home. We were so excited; at last we were going to have a home of our own again.

As I mentioned, Father travelled around a lot with his work and more so after he had been promoted to a foreman. Mother was always concerned for his safety, especially during the air raids and in places where they were facing most of the bombings. So she was most relieved when the war was over and she didn't have to worry any more.

I used to love the weekends and holidays when Father was at home.

So you can imagine the devastation it brought into our home one Saturday morning. The night before, we had all gone to the railway station to meet my father off the train, but he did not arrive, so mother said, "He must have caught a later train." On the way back home, we bought fish and chips and a portion for Father which Mother said could be warmed up later. We went to meet the next train but he was not on that one either. Mother said: "Perhaps he has decided to travel in the morning." We did not have a phone (not many people did have one then) so he would not have been able to contact us.

The next morning Barbara and Reg were out, Grandpa was working, Grandma, as usual, was in her room and I was upstairs practicing the violin.

I heard the doorbell ring and stopped to listen wondering who it was. I heard men's voices, then Mother cry out, I ran downstairs. There were two policemen in the room.

"What's wrong?" I cried.

"Your father has been killed", she said.

I was stunned. My mind went blank. I was eleven years old then and I struggled to take it in.

"Dead"

Did this mean I would never see him again? How dreadful never to see him again. My mind went back to the last time I had seen him: Mother was taking us on the train to Nottingham to go shopping. Father was sitting on his push bike at the level crossing waiting to wave to us as the train went through. We had all spotted him and waved like mad; that was my last memory of him.

When the police had gone, Mother put her arm around me saying: "You are my last hope - the last hope I've got." To this day I do not know why she said that. Only that, from that moment on, I felt responsible for Mother, as being the only hope she had. I took it, that, from now on, I was to look after her now Father was not there.

Mother had to go to London to identify the body where she learned in more detail how Father had been killed. He had called in the late afternoon at his London office for his wages and, as they were not quite ready for him, he decides to go for a drink while he waited.

While in the pub, he noticed a couple of Irishmen were having an argument with a British soldier and as the soldier got up to leave, the Irishmen followed him out. Once outside, they started beating him up. My father saw what was happening and went out to try and stop them. One of the Irishmen turned on my father and punched him so hard, he fell to the floor and hit his head on the pavement. The impact broke his skull and killed him. The soldier was left unconscious but survived and was able to tell Mother and the police what happened. There was a court case; his killers were convicted of manslaughter, but I don't know what the penalty turned out to be, if any.

While Mother had gone to London to identify the body, one of the church people had asked us children out to tea, I know they were concerned for us and were being kind. But being with other people was the last thing I wanted.

When we got there, I kept escaping to the back of their greenhouse to be alone. Crying didn't heal the pain and the emptiness I felt at that time. I had only lived with my father for five years but he had brightened up my life and now it was darker than it had ever been before. It was as if the curtains had become drawn and the light gone out; this was an experience I would never forget: the hollow and emptiness I felt along with the concern for Mother.

Mother now had to decorate the cottage all on her own and I don't know how many times she would sit at the bottom of the step ladder crying. She wanted me to sleep with her at night and I would often hear her crying. I knew why she was crying, but I felt I had to ask her in case she thought I didn't care. I would say: "Why are you crying?" They were such dark days for all of us. Sometime later, I found the fish and chips we had saved for dad in the food safe. I found this very emotional and knew I had to throw them away before Mother found them.

Mother was too ill to work for sometime after Father was killed. Remember, there was no such thing as government benefits in those days, all Mother got was a widow's pension of ten shillings a week which today would be around 50p. Of course the value of money was a lot more then, but 50p a week was nowhere near enough to buy all the food and clothes our family needed.

As mentioned before, Mother had come back to the Lord and- continued in the same kind of church as we had been introduced to while we were in London and before all this had happened. As a family we were committed to regular church meetings and to the church's teachings. Looking back, at that time I still felt the fellowship had biblical and sound teachings. I especially loved the people there and the kindness that they showed us.

One particular family I owe so much to was a Mr and Mrs Purse and their two small children. Mr Purse used to be the head of a fox hunt until he came to faith. He was like a spiritual father and a natural father to me after losing my own. We children would be free to walk into their home any time of day. He would talk me through biblical and other concerns I had, and set me on fire spiritually.

Yes, we were poor financially, never having all we wanted, but God gave us all we needed. We had clothes handed down to us, fruit and vegetables from one of my farm friend's parents, Mother would buy sheep and pigs heads to make brawn, and there was plenty of wild rabbit to be had. We would keep our own rabbits for meat along with chickens; all making a really tasty stew or roast. This experience taught me that, provided we are wise with our money, God will always provide. He never once let us down.

The cottage we were living in had no water in the house. There was a tap in the back yard shared with our next-door neighbour. The only toilet we had was at the bottom of the yard. There was no electricity in the house, just gas lights downstairs and none up, so, again, it meant taking a candle to bed each night. There was no bathroom but, in the yard, was a shed we called the washhouse where we bathed.

The washhouse had a brick copper we would have to fill with water from the tap in the yard, then light a fire under this copper to heat the water. The hot water would then be ladled out into an old zinc bath and we would all bath in the same water. So as you can imagine, bath night would only be once a week. The same procedure would be carried out for wash days with the washing all done by hand in the bath tub using a scrubbing board.

The newer houses were much more modern. They had bathrooms with hot and cold water inside and electric lights - just like the house we had lived in, in Bournemouth and Sutton before we came to sleepy little Oakham.

We had two rooms downstairs: the front room and the kitchen that was large enough to be lived in most of the time. Again there was the old black leaded fireplace with an oven and boiler either side of it. It was cosy on a cold winter's evening sitting round the coal fire, reading, knitting, making peg rugs or playing board games. Only the well off could afford television and even these were still in the primitive stages and were a strain on the eyes. Of course, we would never be allowed one as Church members, as already mentioned; no radio either. I am sure we were not disadvantaged without them as we made our own fun and I never felt I was missing out at that time. In fact, we had lots of fun on my friends' farms helping gathering in the harvests, milking the cows, driving the tractor, riding the horses, shooting the rabbits as they ran out of the corn or going *rabbiting* with ferrets.

We learnt a lot more about nature and things that mattered. My very best friend was Joan Rains. Her father also kept hunting horses and she and I would get up early in the morning, dress up in riding gear when the hunt was on, and follow them on horseback. We were never allowed to enter the hunt but we could follow.

Sir Henry Tate, the owner of Tate and Lyle Sugar Company, would be head of the hunt. He would often come over and asked if we were enjoying ourselves or how we were getting on. By the way, all this rubbish about the dogs tearing the fox to pieces is just not true. The fox is shot long before that can happen. The farmer would lose so many birds once a fox got into his henhouse, killing more chickens than it took away. It was almost as if they killed for the sake of it. Foxes had been known to attack the lambs too, so I was quite happy to watch them being hunted and killed as soon as possible, but not that they should have a prolonged death.

The Trauma

Father's death happened during the summer holidays and going back to school was really hard. Barbara was in the senior school so I can't really say how she was getting on, but my brother Reg. and I were still in the junior school with the same headmaster, Mr. Biggs, and we were finding it very difficult. We were still coping with Father's death and Mr Biggs was not helping. He was not only prejudiced against London *refugees*, but Christians too. There was a film on in the cinema and he had arranged for the school to go and see it. Mother sent a note saying she would rather we were excused. Well, that stirred up a hornet's nest.

First he made my brother and me go to each classroom, stand in front of the children and tell them we did not believe in going to the pictures. From then on we were regarded as outcasts and the children would chant, "Old unbelievers!" at us. Of course, an unbeliever to us meant someone who did not believe in the Lord Jesus Christ, but to them, we did not believe in going to the pictures.

Mother went down to Mr Biggs' house one evening to talk to him about the way he was treating us and she left a Christian book with him. How I wished she had not done this or left the book with him, for the next morning, he called me out.

"Andrew", he bellowed. This was my maiden name.

"Andrew", he called again. "Out here!"

"What am I in for now?" I thought.

"Stand over there so everyone can see you", he continued.

Then he addressed the class. "This girl's mother came to see me last night. She tried to convert me, she quoted the Bible to me, stuff I could read myself, if I wanted to. She gave me this book, stuffed full of religious notions. Would you read a book like this?"

"No sir", they all replied.

"Neither will I", he said and threw the book at me.

Still feeling the loss of my father, home seemed to have become even darker and more mournful. While trying to comfort Mother, I now had this almost unbearable situation at school to deal with.. I dared not tell Mother how I felt as she had enough to deal with herself, still mourning the loss of Father. Another reason for not telling her was the likelihood she would she only make matters worse by going to see Mr Biggs again.

I remember praying one night after feeling so down, and telling the Lord how lonely I was and how much I was hurting, when suddenly I felt as if his presence had filled the bedroom. It was so real that I opened my eyes and looked towards the door. I could not see Him, but it was as if I knew in which part of the room He was.

My heart lifted. "You're here", I said.

I didn't need to see Him because I could feel Him; His presence was removing the pain I had been feeling. He lit up my life. I was still only eleven years old but have never forgotten the experience. It wasn't that I had expected Him to come, I hadn't asked Him, He just came. I knew from then on, he saw and knew all that was going on, and He was there with me through it all.

Of course, the persecution didn't end there. I have since learnt that God does not always take you out of the situation but gives you the power and encouragement to rise above it, just as he did that night.

Mr Biggs continued his campaign against us. Mother stopped us from attending any scripture lessons after Mr. Biggs told us that the Bible stories were not true stories. This got him going again, and whenever scripture lessons were being taught, I had to sit on my own and learn the Roman Catholic catechism off by heart. Again, I did not tell Mother for fear she would have something else to say to him, and I think he did it just to get one over on her. I have always thought it strange that, although I was able to recite that catechism off by heart at the time, I could not remember it once I left school, yet, I can still remember poems and other things I learnt at that age. I can only ever remember the first line:"I believe in the virgin Mary" ... nothing else comes back to me.

You may wonder what I was still doing in junior school at the age of eleven. Let me explain: In those days you took what was called the 11+ exam where you either passed to go to the grammar school if you did really well or, with a lower grade went to what we called the Central School. If, however, your grade was not high enough for either, you stayed in junior school until you left school. You would be looked on then as a dropout, although these days we accept that many children have other skills apart from just academic learning. There were many dyslexic children in those days that were never identified as such.

However, when the time came to take the exam, my name was not called out as a participant and when I approach the headmaster about this his reply was: "You are a Londoner so you have to sit the exam in London."

I knew I was never going back to London; my home now was in Oakham. The result was I never sat any exam and, while the other children were going off to their different schools, I was placed with those children who had taken the exam but failed to achieve good enough grades to progress. So I was left in class with these children; still in the junior school and still under the rule of Mr Biggs. You can guess my disappointment.

The teacher in that class used to say: "I can't understand why you are here" and I would explain to her that I had never taken the exam.

When teachers were away they would use me to teach the younger ones to read and write. I used to love doing this. I would be responsible for the whole class and would use the teacher's desk. How different things are today. I was going on for twelve then.

I continued in that class for the next twelve months. In the meantime, Mother had been in touch with the local authorities, highlighting the fact that I had not had the chance to take the exam. Then one day the headmaster came to me saying, "Andrews, do you want to take the exam?" I guess the authorities must have contacted him, so at last I had the opportunity to move on.

Yes, I passed, but not with a grammar-school-grade. Remember, I was not one of those pupils Mr Biggs had been preparing, and, moreover, my moving between different schools didn't help my education. I probably would not have got through to the grammar school anyway as my spelling has always let me down and they were very hot on spelling then. I remember the times I had to stay in after school to learn my spellings. But it wouldn't be long before I had forgotten how to spell the same word again.

So the following summer I made it to the Central School a full twelve months behind the rest of my age group. I found it really difficult to catch up with the others. Most of the time I would not know what the lessons were all about and it seemed worse than the school I attended in Formby.

I was very conscious of my damaged hand and tried to hide it from my new class mates and this, along with my stuttering that I was trying to overcome (it was improving but I was still afraid to talk), coupled with my strict Christian upbringing, I'm sure you will understand, didn't help my self-confidence at all.

The headmaster at my new school was much more open minded than Mr Biggs had been, and my class mates were not all the same ones that had been with me at my junior school. Many came from the surrounding villages and were fresh to me. They all seem to have interests other than pick on me because I was a Christian, and all the other things I was worrying about. Although I was still getting quite a bit of stick from those that knew me from our old school.

Remember me telling you how my father had contracted tuberculoses (TB) and how two of his brothers had died from it? Well, Mother always seemed to fear that my brother and I would develop it and she would continually keep referring to things that we did or things that we didn't do that might bring the disease on. For instance, she would always tell me that if I did not hold my shoulders back, I would get TB. If I didn't go to bed early, I would get TB, or if I didn't keep myself warm, or if I didn't eat properly and so on and so on. It became a threat that if we didn't do as we were told, this would happen. I remember my teacher in the junior school asking me if I had shoulder braces on because I was trying so hard to hold my shoulders back. "Mother said if I did not hold my shoulders back, I would get TB." I replied.

"Quite right", the teacher said.

I would only sleep on my back at nights because that way, my shoulders would be back, but if I lay on my side, they would be curled over. Eventually I truly believed I had developed this dreadful disease and I was going to die.

I dare not tell my mother because I thought it was my fault and I must have done one of those things she had warned me about although I had no idea what it could have been that had caused me to develop TB. I really thought I was not going to live, but dare not tell anyone. Everything I did had the shadow of death on it. While doing my house hold duties, I would say to myself: "I won't be doing this much longer." When with friends and family, my thoughts would be: "You don't know it, but I'll soon be gone." I remember Oakham swimming pool was opposite the Cemetery so that every time I went swimming, I would wonder how long it was going to be, before I would be in there.

I started having panic attacks. If I was sitting in a room and I couldn't see a window open, I thought I could not breathe and I'd have pins and needles from my head to my toes. My body would go ridged. This would happen to me quite a number of times during our church services with the result that I would need to be taken outside. At other times, I would feel faint and everything I looked at would seem so very small, hazy and far away and I would wonder if I was at the point of death. Nobody had any idea why this was happening. I knew, but would never say it, "It was because I was dying". I sat in class trying to get my breath, although I was breathing, it would not satisfy my need and I would panic. Other times I would have to sit up in bed during the night trying to catch my breath. "Am I dying now?" I would ask myself. As I said, I kept all this to myself; it was no use upsetting others, least of all Mother, who had enough to worry about.

Of course I never had TB. As time proved, it was all in the mind but I dare say I would have got over it quicker if I had shared my concerns with someone else who may have convinced me it was all in my imagination.

The reason I have added the account of this experience is to help others who, like me, are also convinced of something that is just in their mind and not a fact. I learnt that the mind can play all sorts of tricks and we can become over occupied with self. The best remedy, I found, is serving others and their needs, because that takes me away from self occupation, something of which I have to continually remind myself. I can't remember how long this phase lasted or how I got over it but, at the age of fourteen, I was getting less and less of these panic attacks.

Now, at fourteen, I was becoming fed up with being different from the others at school. They would talk about film stars, pictures they had seen, things they heard on the radio and places they would go to that I could not. These were all conversation I could not enter into. I wanted to be popular so I began to hide my Christianity in order to become more popular at school. As my circle of friends began to expand, I was being invited to their houses for birthday parties, and they would even ask me to come back at lunchtime early so that we could have a good laugh together. Now, after all the persecution I had received through my school days in Oakham, I was being accepted and making friends. I was able to reveal the person I really was instead of cowering behind my disability and worrying about my Christian principles. Of course, I still continued going along to all the church services. There would have been uproar in the house if I hadn't.

Christianity was not so important to me now. My friends meant more. Although I never digressed from the things that the church taught me were wrong, such as, going to the cinema and the like, I did hide this private life from those at school.

As a Christian, my path at times had been rough and stony, bringing persecution from teaches and other children. Now I was enjoying being accepted. All this has helped me to fully understand how much it means to teenagers to be accepted among their peers.

So my walk with the Lord had discontinued and I even began to question in my own mind the existence of God. What if there was no God? That question, if I let it linger, would make me feel so miserable

Barbara and I left school when we were fifteen, Barbara went on to learn dressmaking and I shorthand and typing. I was employed as the receptionist at an accounting firm in Oakham. My typing was done with one hand and one finger as it still is today, but I was fortunate because my boss had one of his arms blown off during the war and kindly showed me all the shortcuts. One of them is to tie a piece of string from the space key to the floor, making a loop to put his foot through, then operating the space bare with his foot, Mind you, I could never type more than twenty-five words a minute, but I enjoyed my job and it was good to be bringing home some money. Even though Mother had started working again, money was still short. I can remember the first pair of new shoes I bought, they cost me two pounds - can you imagine. I could not stop looking at them. We rarely had anything new.

Two years after this, when Barbara was seventeen, she started seeing a lad called Frank and it wasn't too long before they decided they wanted to marry, but, at seventeen, Barbara had to get Mother's consent. You had to be eighteen to marry without your parents' consent in those days.

Frank was not a Christian and even if he had have been, he would have had to belong to our church so Mother would not give her consent. I'm afraid Mother did not handle the situation very well. There were beatings, punishments and shouting matches which seem to make Barbara more determined to marry him and she eventually took Mother to court to get permission; which the courts granted. I felt sorry for both of them but more so for Barbara because I felt Mother had driven her away. I've learned that love conquers more than the hard-line. In the end, Mother turned her out and she went to live with Frank's mother until they were married.

None of us went to their wedding.

I missed Barbara so much. I knew she was living in Leicester and wanted so badly to see her again, so that when she wrote to ask me if I could arrange to meet her at a certain place in Melton Mowbray, I had to find a way of getting their so Mother would not find out.

I had been going to night school in Melton Mowbray, and thought if I was to tell Mother I had to take an exam on this particular day, she would not suspect I was meeting Barbara instead. So I wrote a note, making out it was from the college I was attending, asking me to take this exam on that particular day. I posted it off to our address. I made sure Mother saw me open the letter, and then I showed it to her. I think she must have guessed there was something fishy about the letter although she never said anything, but she did say she would come with me. How I panicked! How could I put her off? I couldn't; I just had to think of some excuse to cancel our meeting. The only way out was to say I had a bad headache. I think mother believed me, or did she...? Whether she did or not, we didn't go.

All I could think about that day was Barbara waiting in Melton Mowbray for me to turn up, but there was just no way I could let her know I wouldn't be there. We didn't have mobile phones or text messaging then. The real sad thing was that she never knew why I didn't turn up until thirty-four years later. In all that time, I never saw or heard of her again.

From Oakham to Morecambe

There was yet another surprise: My brother and I never knew Mother had a brother until he turned up at our front door one day. Mother was out and I answered the door to a tall, good-looking stranger on the step.

"I'm your uncle; Uncle Wilfred" he said.

My brother Reg was at home so I felt safe to let the stranger in. I suppose during Mother's sixteen years away from her family she would not have wanted everyone to know where she was, but now she was back home and in the fellowship, he must have found out where she was and had come all the way from Morecambe to see her. This was the first contact we had with him or even knew of him.

From then on he seemed to take responsibility for Mother and we began to look up to him as a father figure and even to love him as such. He was single when we first met him but not long after he brought this attractive lady, as we thought, for us to meet and not long after that, he married her. Her name was Elsie. Uncle was thirty-six years old then but more about him later.

Now, more upheaval. The local council decided they wanted to redevelop the area that our cottage was in. They wanted to build new and modern homes and offered Grandpa £400 for our cottage, which was a disgrace. He did try to fight for more money but with no success.

There was now a lot of discussion and decisions to be made as to where we were going to live. We had been living rent-free while Grandpa owned the cottage, but if we were to have one of the new houses, then we would have to pay rent. There were never any handouts from social services then.

Eventually our recently discovered uncle suggested we went to Morecambe to live there with him. He and his wife had a three-storey house, which they let out as flats, with the china shop they owned underneath. We were offered the top flat, which comprised of a living room, a kitchen and three bedrooms. The bathroom was shared with the others in the house but just to have a bathroom again, was bliss. There were electric lights, water we didn't have to go down the yard for, hot water from a tap and, at last, an inside toilet again!

So, with Oakham and all our friends left behind us, we up and left and went to Morecambe. Another new world opened up with new friends to make, which after you have left school, is not quite so easy.

Uncle by now had two baby boys, Neville and Graham, and it ended up being my job to look after them while he and Auntie managed the shop below. That was until I found suitable employment myself.

The first people we met in Morecambe were those of the same church origin as those we had left in Oakham. Uncle took us there that first Sunday. There were not many young people, just two little girls, five and seven, and two little boys about the same age. There were two older boys about my brother's age, fourteen or fifteen but I was disappointed there were no girls my age.

Our gatherings were always referred to as meetings and never services. We never called our meeting rooms, churches or chapels, probably to disassociate ourselves from other denominations. So instead of saying we are going to Chapel or Church, it would always be: we are going to the meeting.

By this time I was sixteen years old. We had settled in to our new home and I eventually found employment in one of the Post Office Departments, sorting savings certificates into numerical order.

Sorry to say, this employment ended when I was called into the office one day and told I had not used up all my sick leave and I needed to take it within a certain time and when would I take it?

I told them I would let them know once I had spoken to my mother. My mother whose response was: "You don't take sick leave if you are not sick; that's unrighteous!"

I relayed this back to my boss and was told they no longer needed my services. Sacking someone, in those days, was much easier than it is today. It seemed everyone took the allotted sick leave whether they were ill or not and my mother's view on that was just not welcome.

I had set my heart on being a children's nurse after I left school but found no one would employ me with a hand I could not use. I was always good at maths at school and remember the boys often flicking bits of paper with the end of a ruler with "Give us the answer" written on them. In some cases, it was not just a matter of giving the answer but writing the whole sum out to let them see how I'd come to that answer. In such cases, I would just ignore them.

So, as maths was my strongest subject, I joined the accounts department at Williamson's Lino factory in Lancaster. This meant I had to cycle six miles there and then six miles back home every day. Work commenced at seven in the morning so I left home at six and finished at five.

The factory was the other side of the River Lune, so I would have to put my bike onto my shoulders and carry it up two flights of steps, across the bridge and down again the other side. Otherwise I would have had to ride through the town and along the quayside to get to work, which was much further.

After leaving my friends in Oakham behind and meeting with the Christians in Morecambe, I repented of my rebellious ways and settled down; trying to walk the Christian path that I thought was pleasing to the Lord.

I worked in the Lino factory for over eight years and it was not too easy holding on to your faith among some of the temptations I was faced with. For instance, boys were becoming a problem. I did not want to marry a boy that was not a Christian or even one that did not belong to my church fellowship as I would have been expelled from the church. I thought of what Barbara had gone through and that was enough for me. I also knew it would be an unequal yoke and was not God's plan for me to do so, but I did like the attention the boys gave me. I would flirt with them in the office or on the shop floor but would not let them take me out. One young man came to question my mother after I told him I was a Christian and as he was not, I couldn't form a link that would not last. Of course, the other factor I would never mention to them was that I would have been withdrawn from by my church if I was ever found to have formed any relationship with someone who did not belong to the Fellowship.

You can possibly guess my mother's answer. Needless to say, he never approached me again after that! Where could any boy take me? I did not go to the pictures, I did not go dancing, I did not go to the fairground, or football matches. I felt in all this that I was making the right decision because in my mind, my church was always right.

However, eventually I did succumb to one young man named Paul. He worked in my office, and I had to repeatedly refuse his advances and explain my reasons for turning him down. I explained to him that because I was a Christian and he wasn't, there was not much point starting something that was not going to lead anywhere. But this did not stop him persistently asking, day after day. Eventually I gave in and I said I would go out for a cycle ride with him just the once, thinking that it would be the end of it and he would let go. So the next Saturday afternoon we arranged to meet.

Of course Mother did not know. I kept it from her, but once I had given in to him that first time, it was easy for him to persuade me again to go the next Saturday and it wasn't long before I was looking forward to these times when we would be on our own together. We would always end up sitting on the shore or on the crag together. Mother thought I was just out on my own for a cycle ride. I would take a book with me so she would think I would be cycling or reading in some quiet spot.

I think at the time, I was in love, for whenever we were apart; I could not wait to see him again. I was now in a situation I could not get out of. I was deceiving my mother and the church and I felt I was falling deeper and deeper into something that was going to end in disaster. It had also become far too difficult for me to end the relationship. We seriously talked of running away together as Mother would never give her permission for me to marry. I had seen it all before with Barbara. Beside all that, I had heard of people who had married non-Christian partners only for it to end in disaster. Did I want this to happen to me?

One part of me desperately wanted to finish the relationship with Paul so that I could put things right with God, and Mother. Another part of me wanted desperately to carry on with things as they were and to suffer the consequences later.

Just going out with a boy who did not belong to the fellowship was enough for me to have been excommunicated, let alone talk of marriage, so I was only too aware of what the consequences would be.

It was as if I was caught in a web, struggling to be free and not having the willpower to do it.

Night after night my prayer would come from Psalm 77: "I cry out to you, my God, for help. I cry out to you, O God to hear me."

Another was Psalm 121: "I will lift up my eyes to the hills. Where does my help come from? My help comes from the Lord, the maker of heaven and earth" But no help seemed to come. I had told this lad so many times that I was a Christian and would never be able to marry him, thinking that would help, but he would only say he would talk me round. On several occasions I told him it was finished and I could not meet him again, but because we work together, it was too difficult and within a couple of weeks we were back together again.

I would sit in the church meetings thinking I was the most deceitful Christian on earth. To me, at that time, my church was wonderful and I considered them to be people who were always right in their doctrines.

Separation from the world was so strongly emphasised by taking such Scriptures as:
"Touch not the world or the things that are in the world."
"Be not unequally yoked with unbelievers" and
"Come out from among them and be ye separate says the Lord."

I have a better understanding of these Scriptures now, although I still hold on to them but not in quite the same way as I understood them then. So you can imagine how my friendship with Paul was such a great weight on my shoulders.

Eventually I came to a decision. I could no longer live as I had been doing and I must give up the Christian path. I knelt down by my bed and covered my head with the bed clothes, (I always do this when I'm praying in earnest) telling God I could no longer live this life. I was giving up. I was not good enough and I never would be. I was leaving my church.

As I got off my knees, the first line of a poem from one of Mother's poem books came to me:

See I have chosen thee, thou shalt be mine,
In changeless bonds of love divine,

Called while thy youth is strong,
While yet your days long,
From earthly love and song
I claim thee mine

Mine by a tender love that holds they heart
When all thy joys are lost and friends depart

That loves thee holds thee yet
When all your friends forget

I claim thee desolate
I claim thee mine

Mine by the strength of love proven in death.
By that long passion borne, that yielded

By sorrow manifold,
By pain, and grief untold,
By death so still and cold,
I claim thee mine

Mine by a living love, proven to day
My eye has marked your onward way.

By all things fair and sweet.
That mark my passing feet.
Where you and I can meet.
I claim the mine.

By F. Morford

With the words of this poem ringing in my ears, I wondered if there could ever be an escape. Jesus owned me. I thought of these words from the Psalm:

"Where can I go from your presence? If I go to the mountain, you are there. If I go to the depth of the earth, you are there."

It seemed Satan was on one side and God on the other, both pulling in opposite directions.

I felt like the lost son in the parable Jesus told. When the son asked for his share of his father's estate, the father gave it to him.

I had been given salvation and *sonship,* through Jesus Christ.

In that parable, the son had gone off into a far country, away from his father's house.

I, too, had gone off, doing and done my own thing, and this was leading me down the same path the prodigal son had gone down.

He began to be in need; his father, in the parable, knew this but did nothing to rescue him.

Had I not been in need and been praying? Yet God had not come to rescue me.

Then I noticed that when the son had reached rock bottom, he came to himself and he says: "I will go to my father."

The story goes on to say, "He [the son] got up and went" The *son* did something.

He made a move in the right direction and, as soon as he moved, the father ran to meet him.

Had I made a move? No I hadn't. I had prayed expecting the Father to rescue me but had done nothing to show Him I was serious.

I had got myself into this situation and it seemed as if I had expected God to just lift me out of it when I was ready to be lifted.

As I look back now, I wonder if God had made it that easy, would I just have drifted into the next temptation that came along and, once again just expected God to do the same for me again? Thankfully, now I can see, God does not work like that. I had to make the first move, just like the lost son.

The father stood and waited. He did not run until the son had made the first move. I imagined God standing and waiting for me to make a move in the right direction and, if I made a move, He would then run to meet me too.

So the next day I phoned the personnel department and asked to be given a transfer to another department. This was something I did not want to do but understood it to be the only way to be released from my feelings and my web of deceit. Within a few days, they phoned me back at my office. But unfortunately, I was out of the office at that precise moment and Paul took the phone call.

I later learned I was offered a position in the wages department but Paul did not tell me. A few weeks later, I phoned personnel again in case they had forgotten. I was told that I was offered a transfer but they had been told that I had changed my mind and wanted to remain where I was. Of course I had to tell them that this was a mistake and that I did still want the transfer. On account of this, I said nothing to Paul until the Friday before the Monday I was due to transfer to my new department. I was afraid he would try and talk me out of it and, I knew it would have been so easy for him to have done this as I really didn't want to leave.

I assumed that now I was not working with him any longer, it would be easier for me to give him up. Yes it was easier except that I now finished work fifteen minutes later than he did and I would find him waiting for me as I came out of the gate so he could walk down the quayside with me. I decided to cycle to work as I used to do, but he would then be waiting for me with his bicycle, all the time pleading with me to meet up with him again.

I tried writing a letter to him explaining again, that, because I was a Christian, I could not carry on meeting with him. He tore it up in front of me. I just couldn't get away from his continual pleading. All this turned out to be instrumental in me losing the feelings I had towards him. Eventually I bought myself a Vesper scooter. That way I could ride out of the factory gates and, although he would be waiting for me, I would just nod my head in acknowledgement and ride on. That is how it all finally ended. The struggle was over, and the joy I felt was unbelievable, I just wanted to keep praising God for his deliverance. I kept singing this verse over and over again...

> Oh what a God how can we sing your praise,
> The hymn's too great for our poor hearts to raise
> But yet we would our adoration bring
> Your spirit lifts us up and makes us sing.

So I learnt that God expects us to make the first move. I think I became a stronger person as a result and I was forever on my guard not to be involved in anything like that again. I learnt never to sit back and expect God to run before you make the first move; let him see you are serious

I discovered, too, that when temptation comes, you need to draw back right at the start, before you get too deeply involved. If you stay too long, Satan will enslave you in his sticky web and you'll find it extremely difficult to break free. With this in mind, and many years later, I wrote the following poem for the young people I was working with.

THE WEB OF LIES

> The Devils like a spider, who spins his sticky web.
> And hides in cracks and crevices and feeds upon the dead.
> His web is so attractive while shining in the sun.
> But mark my words dear reader; you'll be dead before he's done.
> His speech is so persuasive, but folk there is no doubt.
> If unaware of who he is, he's sure to catch you out.
>
> For he will see you coming before you know he's there.
> So young folk just be ready or he'll catch you unaware.

You'll see him in the Broadway and in the city streets.
His conversation starts like this with everyone he meets.

O come into my parlour dear, how could you pass me by.
It's the most attractive parlour child, that ever you could spy.
It's full of dainty morsels to delight the taste of all.
And pleasures by the thousands, if only you would call.

My parlour's decorated in such ways to please the eye.
With gold and silver tinsel, to attract the passer by.
Lights that glitter brightly and candles around the room.
To brighten up your lifestyle and chase away the gloom.

Boys you're strong and handsome and girls you're young and fit.
Like others in their early teens you're full of life and wit,
If only you would join me, we could laugh away the days,
And you could get accustomed to the world and all its way.

The Bible student shakes his head, he knows his wily ways.
He knows the web the devil spins for unsuspecting prey.
He knows that once inside his den, he's sure to make him stay.
And bind him with his sticky web so he can't get away.

And so the student passes by, but Satan undeterred.
We'll wait to lure another soul and Christians are preferred.
So youngsters do not listen when he tempts you to do wrong
What at first looks harmless fun, will not be fun for long.

Remember when you see that web so delicate and fine.
He's hiding in some little hole and watching all the time.
So youngsters do not listen, to Satan you say no.
Turn away and as you do just tell him where to go.

Before we finish let me add, there's hope for everyone.
That's bound in Satan's sticky web and wants to be undone.
Christ came to set the captive free, release from Satan's grasp.
New life is found in Jesus as he takes away the past.

A Struggle Ended

Having at last broken my links with Paul and feeling as if some great weight had been lifted off my shoulders, I decided from then on I would remain single until, or if ever, the right Christian boy came along. I never wanted to go through that struggle again and my future now was in God's hands.

As I have said, if God had made it easy for me, I may have been tempted to go that way again. Who knows? If the father had made it easy for his lost son, he may have left his father's house again.

At this time my relationship with God had never been better and I was quite content to remain single and enjoy what I was experiencing in the spiritual realm. I had realised it is not the gathering together or the fellow church members you meet with, so much as your own personal relationship with God, that brings real joy into your soul. I could sit in church and never have any close relationship with God.

Neither Mother nor anyone else knew anything about the struggle I had been through, or how I had come through it. No one really knew why I had bought myself a Vesper scooter. All that was between God and me: a secret that we shared. I was enjoying this time with Him. He knew my pain. I shared everything with Him that I could not have shared with anyone else. I couldn't wait to be on my own at night to spend time with Him in prayer and conversation.

I can see now, through this experience, how Christ brings us through and how it is possible to rise above painful circumstances and we are able to enjoy a relationship with God that exceeds the pain this life sometimes brings.

Two years later I met a Christian boy from Scotland named Norman while at three-day meeting in Belfast. He was five years older than I was and we spent most of those three days together and then continued to correspond after that. He invited me to come and stay at a friend of his in Glasgow, so that we could meet up again.

His brother lived in America and Norman told me he was going over there for a period of three months. He promised that he would write to me and I would meet his parents when he returned. Nevertheless, I had no letter from him the whole time he was in America, although I did get a phone call from his sister in Glasgow, inviting me to come and visit for the weekend of his return. I was upset, and thought the least he could do if he was interested. was to write now and again.

In the meantime, a Christian family had come to stay in Morecambe with a friend of ours with their two adults sons, John and David and a ten-year-old daughter; all members of the church. Our friend arranged for us to all go out together one evening to view the Morecambe illuminations. As we walked along the promenade and around the lights in the Park, I began to notice John was always beside me. I thought that maybe it was because we were about the same age so I did not worry about it too much; after all, I was waiting for Norman.

We all went out together again on the following Saturday, up on the crag overlooking the sea, John was always near, teasingly putting grass down my back and chatting to me. As we walked down the crack and along the promenade to the car, we held hands. Other boys had held hands with me before, so, again, I didn't make a lot of it. After all, I had Norman.

While walking together, we met one of the church members coming towards us and I didn't want him to see us holding hands, as there was nothing to it. So I tried to pull my hand away but John held fast and would not let go. I remember saying to myself: "Oh no, this lad means business!" And I was right.

I could not sleep that night. my head was in spin, what should I do? Had I to make a decision between John and Norman? After all, Norman had not written and perhaps he was no longer interested. I had a lot of thinking to do, but I did not realise how quickly John was going to move.

The pressure was building up and I remember my uncle saying to me, "Don't lead him up the garden path if you don't want him." Little did he know the tumult I was going through.

I had been saving a week's holiday from work to go to Glasgow when Norman got back, but, as he had not written, I was not sure if I was still invited. Now John had asked me to come to his home town of Luton for the very week I had saved.

Norman was rough and ready and a good laugh to be with while, on the other hand, John was very caring and kind and a lot more sensible than Norman. They were both so different and I had feelings for both. I prayed hard that God would help me to choose the right one. In the end, John moved so fast I hardly had time to make a decision and found myself in Luton the very week I had saved to go to Glasgow.

I did not have the heart to let Norman know, when he returned, that I was no longer interested so, I phoned one of my friends in Glasgow (the family I had stayed with when I had last visited Norman) and told them I was seeing a boy from Luton knowing they would tell Norman this news when he got back. I never did find out why he did not write. Was it because he too was no longer interested? I was more than happy with John.

Mother and I had lived on our own after my brother, Reg had joined the Kings Own and home life had been very quiet without him. We had no car to go around in but the beach was only a ten-minute walk away, although we did not often go there unless visitors came to us for a holiday. Only then would we go down on the beach or take them to the little bays we knew. I suppose these outings were one of our highlights of the summer months.

My biggest highlight each year would be the three-day meeting in Belfast where church members would put as many young people up in one hotel as possible with only a few adults to keep their eye on us. This was great fun. We would all go out at night around the streets of Belfast almost always ending up at a chip shop sharing bags of chips and bottles of lemonade. Pubs were out of bounds, of course. You might say this doesn't sound much fun, but for me, just being with young folk my own age, was great.

So you can imagine the joy that I felt when I went to stay with John's family. Here was a real family: dad and mum and children: brothers and sisters John had another sister, Margaret, who was married and had two little boys, Paul and Michael. They lived in Dunstable at the time.

I don't think I had experienced real family life until then. His mother did not go out to work but devoted her time to the family; she was kind and motherly. His father was well versed in the Bible and you never really knew when he was teasing you or when he meant what he said. There was always an open door and folk were not afraid to call at any time of day. There would be a lot of banter going on especially between the young folk. I loved it there. Of course, this may have been something to do with John being there too.

As I've already mentioned, John acted very quickly. We first met in the August, engaged by Christmas and married that next summer. I tried to hold him back as I wanted to be quite sure this was the man I wanted to spend the rest of my life with. He suggested I came to live in Luton before the wedding so that we could get to know each other better. John worked on Saturday and could not get the time off to come to Morecambe on weekends so I was having to do all the travelling and the fare cost a whole week's wages each time I came to see him. If we were to marry, we would need to save.

Moving to Luton meant leaving Mother on her own but I was always thankful that she didn't appear to be too upset, in fact, she encouraged me to go. I remember her joking with John that she had put up with me for over twenty years and it was time someone else had a go.

So John found me accommodation in Luton and I found employment in a finance company, the Vauxhall and General Finance Company.

Most of my evening meals were with John's family and I was treated as one of them, while John treated me like a china doll. I had never been so happy.

We married on 5 September 1959, in Lancaster Register Office, as we could not conduct weddings in our meeting rooms because we were not licenced to do so. In those days, we were not even allowed a white wedding, although this rule changed not long after our wedding. So I had just missed the chance of being married in white, something I have always regretted. Every girl's dream is to have a white wedding. I was married in a navy lace dress: just below the knee in length, a white slip under it, white hat, white gloves, white handbag and navy lace shoes. If you can imagine all that!

We didn't have a reception either. We had a service in the meeting room after getting married in Lancaster registry office. Church members came from around the area to be there and a good number from the Luton gathering turned up. We had tea and sandwiches in the meeting room after the wedding service, then, as many as could, came back to my mother's house for orange juice or tea with a slice of wedding cake. Although church members were not against alcohol in moderation, at that time, neither family could afford to buy it. We didn't need a big reception to be happy. I don't think it would have made us any happier than we were that day. We spent our honeymoon in North Wales; a glorious two-weeks of warm sunshine.

Before we had married, John had sold his car to put down a deposit for a three-bedroom house. In its place, he bought a motorbike and sidecar. The house should have been ready by the time we were back from honeymoon but, as usual, building work ran six weeks behind schedule so we lived with John's family until it was finished.

I continued to work for another twelve months after we were married to help buy those things we needed for the home. We had moved in with just a bed, a kitchen table and chairs, and the living room carpet. Everything else had to wait until we had enough money to buy it. We had more or less got there after twelve months and the house was now fully furnished.

I didn't want to be a working mother; I wanted to have a family where mother stayed at home. My mother had to work to keep bread on the table and it had been pretty miserable for us kids. We would come home from school to a cold and empty house. We would have to light the fire, get the meal ready and then clean up. Mother came home in the evenings exhausted and irritable. You couldn't call it a family life; it was as if we just existed all altogether in the same house, never spending time with each other. If we were ill, Mother never had the time to look after us. We were never washed until we were well enough to get up and wash ourselves. Mother's life centred on bringing in money to keep us. She was on what was known as, piecework. She had a target to reach with the clothes she would machine. If she did not reach her target, she came home with less money at the end of that week. If the target was achieved too often, her employer would set it up higher. To add to this, women were not paid anywhere near what men were being paid for doing the same job. So it was a constant battle for her to bring in enough to keep us on.

There was no allowance made for sick pay if you ever had to stay off work. Each day you were off, you lost a day's pay. As result of this, my dream was always to have a family like John's where no one was too busy to care for each other.

Like most newlyweds, we had to count the pennies to make ends meet. At times, John would worry as to how we were going to get our bills paid, but I had learnt through Mothers lean times, that God never lets us down. He always provided something out of nothing, or so it seemed. When Mother did not know where the next meal was coming from or when we had grown out of our clothes, or the bills needed to be paid, we found that these needs were always met, so I was confident that God would provide for us as long as John and I were wise with what He had already given us. I think that this is something positive I have learnt since my father's death and, as a result, I am thankful God taught me I could trust Him.

New Ministry with Devastating Results

Although I did not know it at the time, I must have been about a month pregnant when I left work. Strangely enough, a gypsy had come to the door one day and told me I was pregnant and was going to have a son. Of course I didn't believe her, but I did hope it was true. Well, it wasn't long before I found she had been right because eight months later, we did have a son and called him Andrew.

But there is another heartbreaking story to tell before Andrew arrived: I really don't know how to start. Unless I explain at this point, a little of the history and doctrines of the, church you will never understand what came next. So please bear with me.

Ever since this church was founded in the eighteen hundreds, there have been many deviations and breakups, mainly through doctrinal differences.

Now, we were in the process of suffering another split. This involved the rule of keeping yourself separated from the world by not even eating with anyone who did not belong to our fellowship. This doctrine is based on the Scripture: "With such a one not even to eat." (1 Corinthians 5: 11) Those that took on this ministry were known by others as, "Closed Christians"

We only had one Universal Leader, one that every gathering would look up to and hang on every word he said, just like John and I did. He was considered to be the person to whom God has given His authority and through whom God spoke. This Universal Leader's ministry would be relayed to every gathering around the world, through a printed booklet. We would receive this booklet, known as the *White Book* every week. It was a printed record of all the meetings the Universal Leader had held in different places throughout the week. You obeyed and believed everything the Universal Leader said because we understood it to have come from God.

It was always said that we were the true church and the only right position in the whole of Christendom. We were the only ones to whom God was making His thoughts known.

Purity had to be kept and maintained. As we were the representation of Christ's bride, His church, His assembly, any taint of sin had to be judged and dealt with to maintain this purity. Even if a person who had sinned had then confessed their wrongdoing and repented, they still had to be withdrawn from to clear the assembly of shame.

1 Corinthians 5 is one of the scriptures used to support this ministry particularly verse 11. You will see Paul is saying, "I am writing to you that you must not associate with anyone who calls himself a brother that is sexually immoral or greedy, an idolatry or slanderer, a drunkard, or swindler, with such a man not even to eat."

The next verse goes on to ask what business is it of mine to judge those outside the church. "Are you not to judge those inside? God will judge those outside. Expel the wicked man from among you!"

Paul seems to be saying that we have to judge those believers that are in the church, but God judges those who are not Christians. Of course, as I understand it now, I think Paul is referring to a church member or believer who does not repent or continues with his wrongdoing as the one we need to judge.

Don't get me wrong, people were restored to the gatherings but only after months or years, and only when they were deemed repentant enough to be forgiven and welcomed back into the fellowship again. You could repent over and over, but you never got accepted back until those brothers who were dealing with you, were satisfied that your repentance was deep enough. Such brothers were called the priests. All this is taken from the Old Testament books of Leviticus, Numbers and Deuteronomy, where the priests had to keep looking to see if the "sore" had healed and all the washing and the purifying had been done that was necessary for restoration.

So it is with our church it is a long process of purification.

I now have a different view to the one I had then, although, I am still thankful for those books in the Old Testament, because through them, I see the greatness and the holiness of God and how distasteful sin is to Him. But then, as I read the New Testament, I see that if I confess my sin I am purified by the blood of Jesus and there are no more sacrifices needed to be made, no more washing to be done and no more being put outside the camp as they had to do in the Old Testament days. I see such mercy and such love of so great a God who found a way for me to escape from what should have been my eternal punishment. God himself became my sacrifice, my righteousness and my purification He became as one of us, to bear my punishment and set me free.

> The sinner who believes is free
> Can say the saviour died for me.
> Can look to the atoning blood.
> And say this made my peace with God

But this was not how I viewed it back then as our church to me, were the only ones that were right.

When I first came among the members of this church at the age of eleven, they were not as radical then, nothing dramatic was being said, or demanded, Of course, as already mentioned, we did not do worldly things such as fairgrounds, movies, radio or TV, which I had no reason to question. As far as I was concerned, it was normal for a Christian to distance them self from the world. I was too young to understand all this then. I was there because Mother was there and this was the accepted Christian path and I had no reason to question it.

Then the leadership changed. A new Universal Leader took over the fellowship and the purity ministry was strenuously adhered to, demanding us to be even more separate from the world. This new Universal Leader instructed us that we were not even to eat with anyone we did not "break bread" with (the Lord's Supper). If you had a relation or anyone living with you that was not in the Fellowship, you either had to get them to join the church or tell them to leave your home. Husbands, relations, even young people over a certain age, could not live with you if they were not in the fellowship. Not many people, as I remember, left their homes as most simply joined the church. Whether or not they became true Christians, is not for me to say.

As you can imagine, many did not agree with this new ministry. This caused yet another split as there were members leaving all over the world that did not agree with these new extreme commands.

This was a terrible time. John and I were still in our twenties, not knowing what to make of it all and I suppose, because our church members in Luton were staying together, we did not think too much about it at all. It was not until this doctrine erupted in the Luton gathering that John and I were compelled to either accept or reject it.

We shall never forget that one particular night that devastated our lives so painfully. We were not at all expecting what then took place...

The question of not eating with those who did not take the Lord's Supper with us was bought up by the man who led the Luton congregation, a hard character who rarely showed the spirit of Grace or Compassion. We always felt he was not the right man to be leading our gathering but, because there was no official appointing of leaders, it was very often the one with the strongest personality that rose to the top and took over.

This question of not eating with those not in fellowship with us was raised in such a legalistic way that those, who did not agree with it, got up and stood at the back of the hall. John's father was the first to get up and we watched as the rest of his family followed. Slowly others joined him.

Then John's father gave a speech from the back of the room that I did not think properly demonstrated the spirit of Christ, it seemed to me he was giving vent to his anger rather than trying to put over what he thought to be right and his anger was all directed at this local leader. I could understand John's father's frustration, but it didn't do a lot to convince me that my father-in-law was right.

John grabbed my hand, I turned to him and said, "Don't go".

I knew if we got up to join them at the back of the hall we would have been withdrawn from and I was not yet sure who was right or who is wrong. We needed time to think, were they right? Should we or shouldn't we be eating with those we did not fellowship with?

When John's father had finished his speech he opened the door and walked out and the others that stood with him followed and our hearts sank.

As soon as the meeting was over, we went to find them. They were all meeting at one of their houses, as they opened the door to us, we were welcomed with open arms, and they all seemed relieved to think we had come to join them.

I didn't know at that point if we had really come to join them. Leaving the fellowship was a decision not to be taken lightly, all I knew was here were the people I loved, here were the people I wanted to be with. John and I knelt down to pray with them, well; I sat on a chair as I was too heavily pregnant to kneel.

Each brother prayed in turn, but I didn't feel there was any power in their prayers and thought, if they had made this tremendous step, would God not have shown some approval and power among them. There was also a great deal of talk that I felt was not God-centred; it was more anger at the local leadership.

After leaving them, John and I talked things over and decided, yes, we were going to join them. It was not that we understood whether the latest ministry was right or wrong, but we wanted to be with those we loved in Luton. We knew we would have to leave the church to do this, at the same time we knew we would be cut off from all those who remained in the fellowship.

We went home to phone my mother in Morecambe, to tell her we were leaving the church My uncle answered the phone, and I asked to speak to Mother.

He said," Your mothers in hospital she has cancer and has had to have her breast removed."

I was so shocked, it took a few seconds to get my breath back.

She had evidently kept it from me so as not to worry me while I was pregnant.

How could I do this to my mother at a time like this?

If I was to leave the church there would be no more contact between us. She had gone through this with Barbara and now, when she needed me the most, I would not be there.

My mind immediately went back to the day we received the news of my father's death and how Mother had said I was her only hope. If the church were right in this latest ministry, how responsible was I to God in doing such a thing? I had to disregard my personal feelings and seek God's will.

I came off the phone, beside myself. Where could I turn? Whichever way I looked, there was only sorrow. There was no escape from it. For days John and I would be crying, we couldn't eat or sleep. We knew we had to make a decision. While we were making this decision, we stayed away from John's family and the church meetings,

During our absence from John's family and the church services, I think John's father thought we had gone back to the church with its latest rules and he became really angry with John. John managed a shop just across the road from his father's house, and he came home one day telling me that he had to lock the shop door as his father was behaving very angrily, pacing up and down outside of the shop. I can understand how his father felt because I know what we were going through and we all react in different ways, but it didn't help us in making our decision.

Eventually, we decided to go and see an old brother in the neighbouring town whom we held in very high regard for. John and I prayed together before we knocked on his door, we asked the Lord to help us to do the right thing whatever the outcome. We were able to tell him exactly how we felt about the brother that had taken the lead in Luton and how badly he had treated those that had left. His reply was:"You don't let personalities get between you and God. That is the only advice I am giving you."

After we left him, we had to admit he was right; a lot that had been said and done involved personal feelings. Then we remembered we had not spoken to him about his thoughts on the latest ministry of not eating with others who were not in our fellowship. We had been so wrapped up with our feelings against our local leader that we had forgotten the main issue.

On the way home, we talked over our conversation with the our elderly friend and then we began to remove the personalities and personal feelings towards our local leader and just consider what was really wrong with us being more separate from the world, bearing in mind those Scriptures our church based this doctrine on.

I was also being heavily influenced to stay in the fellowship, knowing Mother needed my care and did not need the sorrow of losing us, while recovering from her operation. You have to remember that, having such an operation in those days was much more complicated than it is today and not many patients survived.

Mother's illness definitely played a big part in persuading us to stay with the church and its new doctrine and, as time went on, reading and listening to the ministry, we became convinced (wrongly, of course) that we had done the right thing but, as you can imagine, it was tough going as all those we really loved, were missing. They had all left and we could no longer associate with them. It would be twenty-one years before we were able to contact them again.

John's married sister and her husband, who were part of the Rushton fellowship, and not involved in local administration, helped us to settle down again by telling us it was not wrong to put a greater distance between ourselves and the world. I remember Reg at that time, reassuring us that God always lead His people through one man, just as one man, Moses, had lead the Israelites through the wilderness to the Promised Land.

Even now, the pain and emotions return as I go over this with you. Although things fade over time, they never leave you. We never saw John's mother again, she died of cancer fifteen years later. John's younger sister phoned to tell us she was dying, we asked permission from the church to go and see her. We felt we had to ask for fear we would be excommunicated if it was discovered that we had visited her without their knowledge. The answer given was "No."

We knew then, if we went, we would be withdrawn from, and, by this time we had five children to think about, all still in our fellowship meaning any disobedience on our part would have split the family up. As you can imagine, this situation added to the pain John's mother must have endured and the hurt we were feeling too, not being able to go and see her. John wept for days. I had stuck by my mother when she had cancer and now John was facing the same situation, with the added burden of keeping our family together. She died with him never having seen her again. It is still painful to think and to know now, that it was all so unnecessary. I have come to realise just how strong their influence and how brainwashing can override compassion and common sense and how we were totally caught up in it.

But all we had gone through in losing John's family was just a shadow of what we had to go through twenty-one years later, which we will come to later.

Our Five Children

All the aforesaid took place in the April and May of 1961. Andrew was born on 1st. July 1961 after a difficult labour, septicaemia, a temperature of 106 and hallucinations. I was too ill to enjoy the wonder and thrill of our firstborn, it was not until I began to recover that I began to appreciate motherhood for the first time. I really did not think, while I was so ill, that I was going to live to see him grow up.

While I had this infection I was kept in isolation and the nurse assigned to me was not allowed to attend any of the other mothers or children. Andrew was taken from me until I was well enough to look after him. Thanks to penicillin, I pulled through, although for weeks I was too weak to hold myself up, but we got through it.

Andrew was four-months old when he had his first attack of chronic asthma. It was quite frightening, never having seen it before, but that first attack was not the end of it all. At six-months old he had another attack, we phoned the doctor during the night but he did not come until first thing in the morning. As soon as he saw Andrew, he phoned through to the hospital to have an oxygen tent ready, and took him to the hospital in his own car, worried he was not going to get him there in time.

Andrew got over that one only to have another attack four weeks later. The doctor had called just two days previously to see if he was all right, so this time he accused me of panicking and said, "He was fine when I saw him the day before yesterday."

Because of this, he didn't come out to Andrew. I was so worried I called a friend of ours to come around as Andrew kept going blue as he struggled with his breathing, drifting in and out of consciousness. By lunchtime, I had to risk phoning the doctor again but, of course, by that time of day, he was out on his calls. You can imagine the panic I was in. I phoned the doctor again in the evening at his surgery and was told they would book a call or come the following day. I phoned again at 10pm, I was told: "if you think he is that bad, you'd better phone for an ambulance."

I phoned the hospital instead.

Although I knew the only way to get him into hospital was through a Doctor's referral, when they asked if I had phoned the doctor, I said I had, but he wouldn't come out. They told me to bring Andrew down and they would take a look at him. As soon as they saw him, there was panic and they actually reprimanded me for bringing him in, in such a state. I asked them what I was supposed to do if the doctor would not call. They told me I should have phoned the police.

Later they must have got in touch with my doctor, as he came round the following day to see me and to apologise but I was out, so he left a note. We never wanted to see that doctor again and quickly made arrangements to change to another.

The new doctor was so much more helpful. The next attack Andrew suffered, four weeks later, our new doctor came and gave Andrew an adult-size dose of adrenaline and then stayed with him to see if it would work. This, however, didn't work and our doctor explained that it meant he could do nothing further to help Andrew and for any future attacks, he (Andrew) was to be taken straight to hospital. He made arrangements there and then for this to happen.

This was such a great relief, knowing that we no longer had to wait around for doctors to call before we took Andrew in to be treated. The hospital staff found him very difficult to treat as he would not respond to any of the drugs available apart from cortisone which was administered into the veins of his neck, but that was only when everything else had been tried. Sometimes, we would go in to visit and not recognise him, he had been so drugged.

Andrew continued to have these attacks almost every four weeks and we were told by the nursing staff his was the worst case they could ever remember treating. The hospital consultant advised us to have another child as they didn't expect Andrew to survive.

Whenever we would go away, we would have to take a letter from the hospital to let other doctors at other hospitals know how to treat Andrew. One time, we had to go into hospital at Morecambe. The doctor there was really concerned about Andrew and said, "You know we almost lost him."

I explained it is like that every time he goes into hospital.

By the time he was four years old, Andrew had been admitted to hospital thirty-three times. We would pray continually for these attacks to end and that we would have a healthy little boy.

I used to watch other mothers show off their babies and would ask myself: "Why can't I show off my baby like other mums do?" I wanted a healthy baby that John and I could enjoy instead of this struggle to keep him alive, up night after night administering medication, listening to him struggling to breath and then chasing off to hospital in the middle of the night. We would also have to keep people away if they had a sore throat, and not let anyone with a cough or a cold into the house. It was a nightmare.

The doctors at the hospital kept asking me if I had suffered any trauma while I was carrying Andrew, and I had to admit that I had, yet all the time hoping they would not ask me what it was. How could we have explained all we had been through during my pregnancy, they could never understand.

We questioned God as to what he was trying to teach us through Andrew's illness. I think, one of the things we learnt, was: Our children are only loaned to us, they are God's property and He can take them when it is His will to do so. In the meantime, we are responsible for bringing them up to know Him as their saviour. We had this poem framed and put on the wall as a reminder of this.

> What shall we ask for our girls and boys,
> Shall we ask for fame of mere worldly joys?
> For the dear bought wisdom of the schools,
> Or a skilful hand in the use of tools?
> Ah no, our wishes must higher go.
>
> Then the highest hill with its caps of snow,
> And the heart's desire must wider be
> Than the utmost stretch of the boundless sea.
>
> We ask for the blessing of God above,
> And an early sense of the saviour's love,
> An early sense of his wondrous grace,
> And an early start to seek his face.
> The soul that is cleansed by the saviour's blood,
> A heart that is kept by the peace of God.
> Where the very God of peace may dwell,
> His holy secrets of love to tell

Feet that shall walk in the path of light,
And follow the lamb through stress and strife,
That follows on through pain and loss.
They may learn the worth of the Saviour's cross,
A place in their hearts for the word of truth,
And God their guide from their early youth.
Great things do we ask for our girls and boys,
A place in God's universe of joys,
To shine in the land where His son supreme,
And His wondrous Cross is the dearest theme.

Two weeks before our second child was born, Andrew had another attack and we really thought this was the end. We had faced death with him so many times, but in this attack, the doctor had told us that, if the attack did not break in the next few hours, his heart would not stand the strain and he would not pull through.

He was two years and three months old by this time and had been taken into hospital again. His usual doctor was not there, it was a new doctor on duty we had not seen before.

Suddenly a nurse shouted: "His heart's stopped!"

We were rushed out of the room, while equipment was being rushed in. I remember thinking, "it's all over! Lord, we did our best but you want him back."

A few minutes later, the sister came out and said they were doing all they could to try to start his heart again. Sometime later we heard someone shout, "We've got it!"

Did that mean they had got the heart going again? Yes it did, we were so relieved. The Lord had given Andrew back to us, but it had left its mark.

After the trauma and the asthma attack were over, we bought Andrew home only to find he had difficulty walking, so we phoned the hospital to see if he had fallen. We explained he was having trouble walking. I was assured he had not been out of bed, so he could not have fallen while in hospital. We then phoned the doctor, it was not our usual one that came and, after examining Andrew, he passed it off as weakness after being so ill. I told him he had been ill many times before and this had never happened to him. John and I knew that something was not right.

The next day we found he could not walk at all, his legs crumbled under him, he was crying. "I can't get up, I can't get up."

We phoned the doctor again and this time it was our own doctor that came. The consultant's letter from the hospital had not yet reached him and I don't think he was aware that Andrew's heart had stopped. We didn't think to tell him as we never connected these two things together. Eventually, he said, "I don't want to frighten you, but I think it is polio."

We couldn't believe it; we thought polio had been stamped out years ago.

Consequently, Andrew was sent to the hospital outpatients department to see yet another consultant. His notes again were not available or studied as these were still up in the ward he had left the day before. So he was sent to the isolation ward where he remained for the next six weeks. They took a lumbar puncture and then informed us that the polio virus could not be found, but as there was no other explanation, they did not know what else it could be. They kept him there until the incubation period was over. His visitors were restricted to just ourselves and my mother, but we could not enter his room without first putting on protective clothing. John and I had to be immunised against the disease. We were told to keep away from crowded places in case we had contracted the virus. Added to this was the fact that I was more vulnerable to the virus while I was pregnant. Every morning John and I would wake up and ask each other if we felt all right, it was like living under a death sentence.

It was two weeks into our potential incubation period for the virus, that our little girl decided to arrive, I was in labour, I was not ready for it physically, and all that had gone before had taken its toll. I remember saying to myself, "I haven't the strength left in me to go through this…" I relayed these feelings in prayer. And before I had finished, that Scripture came to me: "Be still and know that I am God." It proved to be a quick and easy labour resulting in a beautiful baby girl.

The anxiety then increased, was I going to pass on the polio virus to our new baby? Added to this was the fact that I was not able to go to see Andrew now that I had the baby. I had the same midwife who attended me at Andrew's birth and now for the second time, in my case was again prohibited from attending any other patients in case the virus was passed on.

It was hard to believe that only having been discharged from the isolation ward, they then realised, after finally reading Andrew's medical notes that his heart had stopped. We were told his condition had not been caused by polio after all but brain damage. Andrew's brain had been starved of oxygen for the time that his heart had stopped, and this had the same effect as if he had suffered a stroke.

Andrew did get the use of his right leg back, but his left leg became wasted from the hip down and, eventually, he had to wear a calliper. As he grew older, he underwent several operations to try and stabilise his leg. Eventually, they had to remove all his toes including the big toe so he was left with just a stump for a foot. In later life, he would never let anything get the better of him. He would climb ladders, clean windows, decorating and building; anything practical, he could do it.

My experience with my own arm helped me to understand Andrew's frustration at trying to overcome his disability. He was determined to do whatever others could do and I was very proud to see him battle through this.

Andrew's asthma started to improve as he got older and I think he was fourteen when he had his last visit to hospital but even now has to be very careful when it gets a cold. He went on to be a father with two children, Christy and Luke. Sadly Christy also developed asthma and was continually in intensive care.

Our second child, Sarah proved to be a healthy baby girl with no chest problems, for which we were very thankful, trying to cope with one sick child was enough. I was mindful that, at times, she had to take second place, as our concern and attention was focused on Andrew, but I would try to make it up to Sarah whenever I could.

We were made aware by the hospital consultants that children with asthma sometimes bring on an attack in order to get their own way, and, yes, Andy did try this on one or two occasion but I did not want to be saddled with the spoilt child as well as a sick one, so I refused to give in to his demands. I suppose I had memories of how we were dealt with in the Home; Aunty Clare would make sure we knew that we were under her authority.

I guess most parents will have learned, like I did, that disciplining children is not easy. This would be the easiest thing in the world not to do, but we discipline because we love our children and want the best for them. I guess this mirrors our heavenly Father who corrects and disciplines those He loves. So, when we go through trying times, I ask myself: "What is God saying to me?" I'm sure there's nothing that a Christian goes through that God does not use for their spiritual growth.

The following verse is a good one to remember:

I'm in my father's hand.
Why should I doubt or fear?

My father's hand will never cause
His child a needless tear.

Our daughter proved to be a delightful child and we loved her dearly. I remember, every time she wanted my attention, she would come up to me and say, "My mummy", so how could I do anything else but listen to her with an introduction like that? There are so many happy memories I have of her that would probably be of little interest to you, but are stored in my box of treasured jewels, because that is all I have left of her. I knew only that, as an adult, she married and has six children.

Twenty months after our daughter was born, our third child arrived. He was such a placid and gentle child, original in his thinking, and extremely easy to love. I fill with tears as I write all this, as I think of the close-knit, loving family we once had, now broken.

I don't think we ever had to get cross with him, even when it came to arguing, as children do, he never seemed to get involved, he was always in a world of his own, playing on his own and enjoying his own thoughts. Family disputes were usually between our daughter and Andrew. Again these memories of him are stored in my box of treasures.

Seven years later, John and I decided to have a fourth child. Four months into the pregnancy, we decided it was time to tell the children, they were so excited and were asking all sorts of questions, they could talk of nothing else but the new baby.

But things were not to be. Two weeks later, at sixteen weeks, I was admitted to hospital, haemorrhaging after suffering a miscarriage and the baby had to be taken away. When I came round from the anaesthetic, I was told we had lost the baby. Many mothers have had the same experience and will know how heartbreaking this is.

I will never forget that feeling, part of you is missing, all the excitement and anticipation, and then suddenly it is all gone. I had endured three months of morning sickness only to have nothing at the end of it all. I think I cried for days after. I can quite understand women who have suffered from miscarriage, stealing someone else's baby. I already had three children but it made no difference, so imagine someone who has not had any children, it must be worse for them.

Having to tell the children there was no baby was hard, we felt their disappointment too and had to find ways of cheering them up, when we did not feel very cheerful ourselves.

Two years later, God blessed us when Beth was born. The loss of the past was forgotten when she arrived. There was overwhelming joy and excitement, she was beautiful, and more than made up for the previous disappointment. The children couldn't get over how small her hands and feet were. She gave us a great deal of pleasure and grew up with a very caring personality. Her thoughts for the needs of other people always came before her own, even now devoting her life to caring for the homeless, drug addicts and alcoholics. They all love her as she tries to talk them out of their addictions and speaks to them of the better way of life, through Jesus Christ.

There was a nine-year gap between our second son and Beth and we had no plans for having any more children, but when Beth was five months old, I discovered I was pregnant again. We couldn't believe it as I was still feeding Beth and thought that you could not fall pregnant while you were feeding. I wasn't sure if I could cope with another baby just yet, as I wasn't getting any younger and Beth and Andrew left me feeling very tired. I felt I could do without another baby just then. The doctor confirmed I was pregnant and, at the same time, said something to me that I did not expect.

He said, "Well, God gives and God takes away."

I felt ashamed on hearing him say that because, as one who was supposed to trust God, I should not have been waiting for the doctors tell me this. God was giving us another child, he had a reason and John and I needed to accept this. As time went on, we discovered God had a good reason in giving us this child, as you will see.

Luke was born when Beth was just fourteen months old; all my doubts had gone as to whether I could cope. Now we had this beautiful baby boy, bringing more happiness into our home. The older children were old enough to be able to help out. They would change nappies and feed Beth and do lots of other jobs about the house.

These were good times. Luke grew up to be quite a comic and used to make us laugh a lot. We were so thankful that God had given us the privilege of having Luke. We had learned that nothing happens by chance to those who have committed their lives to God. Luke was a gift that we never expected and made our family complete.

Luke is now married and in time, had two little girls, Diane and Ruth. Several years later, God blessed him with twins, Linda and Joshua.

With such a long gap between our first three children and then the younger two, it was very much like bringing up two families. Saturday was the day we kept as our family day when, whenever possible, we would go out together for the day. One week it would be somewhere that suited the older children, then the following Saturday, somewhere that suited the younger ones.

Our home was always full of youngsters and these were such happy days. As we did not have a TV or radio, we would make up our own entertainment, their friends would come around with their musical instruments and they would make music together. Mealtimes were happy times too, when we would all sit around the table, chatting joking and teasing.

Commands and Demands

As already mentioned, we did a lot of entertaining while in the church, there would be five services on a Sunday and one every evening in the week. Sundays were particularly busy, there would be the breaking of bread at 6am, after that we would come home and have breakfast, then we would be off again to Watford for a Bible reading at 9am, then we would be invited back to the home of one of the Watford church for a snack, maybe twenty or more of us would be invited to that house, then at noon, we would be back in Watford for another service that would finish at about 1pm, then we would travel back home for a rest so we would be ready for a gospel preaching at 3pm in the Luton hall, and then, yet another, at 5pm which would join with the Watford church . That would be five services on a Sunday. The Watford church would come over for this last meeting of the day, and then the Luton church members would invite them back to our homes for an evening meal. We would be allocated about fifteen people.

The following week it would reverse, Luton would do the snacks while Watford would do evening meals. When I say, Watford, that includes all the other gatherings around that area: Hemel Hempstead, St Albans, Radlett and the surrounding areas.

The mid-morning snack on a Sunday would always be something hot and the women would spend a lot of their time preparing. I remember I would be always thinking and planning as to what to prepare for these occasions.

I still had no doubt at this time that the church was doing what was right and we were all pleasing the Lord through the instructions the Lord was giving, through our Universal Leader.

Having already lost Barbara all those years ago, we were now about to lose my brother, Reg. It came up in the ministry that all men had to marry. Well, my brother was single and because there was no sign of him even trying to find a wife, he was accused publicly of going against the Universal Leader. He was made to feel very uncomfortable and not accepted in the church

At that time, my brother was living with Mother in Leicester. Eventually, he left Mother a note saying that he did not fit in because he was not married and was not wanted in the church

For this reason, he had left and did not want anyone to find him. We were devastated. This meant there could no longer be any contact between us and no one knew where he had gone. It would be ten years before we would see or hear from him again, but we will come to that later.

One of the things that John and I could not understand or accept was the amount of whiskey that was drunk among the church members. Whiskey had to be provided with the snacks on a Sunday. Hopefully someone would bring a bottle with them because, with a family of seven and having to provide whiskey for twenty or so people could prove to be quite expensive.

We were told we all had to provide whiskey when we entertained our visitors. At first John and I rebelled, I remember the drinking problem my father had and the manner in which he was killed, so we said we would not have any whiskey in the house.

Eventually we had to give in, after our local leader came around to see us and asked us why we were not providing it? We received quite a lecture from him during which he asked us what we would have given him if he had been around preaching all day, and had come to our house exhausted.

"A jolly good dose of herbs", we replied.

As he was a chemist, he did not take kindly to that remark; herbs were not his scene. Of course, the answer he wanted was whiskey.

However, the next morning, he turned up with a full bottle of the stuff and we were told at that point that if we did not accept it, we would be rebelling against the Universal Leader, and that would have meant being withdrawn from. I do know of at least one brother, personally, who was withdrawn from because he refused to have whiskey in his house. He was asked publicly at one of the meetings if he was free to have it in his house, and his answer was: "No he wouldn't"

He was excommunicated. Whether he had not toed the line over other things, and this was the end of an accumulation of things, I don't know.

When I spoke of my experiences as a child and the results of drink on our family, I was told that, if we had the Holy Spirit, we should be able to control our drink, but I noticed at times, some of the young ones could not and would then be withdrawn from, for being drunk.

When Andrew was sixteen, I became a concerned about the amount he was drinking. We never allowed the children to drink in our home but he would go off with his church friends to other homes, where he would be allowed to drink, or he would sit in cars with them drinking. We can remember two occasions when he bought a friend home that was too drunk to drive to his own home. We called his father to come and take him home. Another time, the same boy, came home with Andrew late one Saturday night and asked if he could stay the night because it was so late. As we were in bed already, we agreed to let him but to our horror, we discovered the next morning, they had both drunk half a bottle of rum each and had been sick everywhere; on the mattresses, the bedclothes and on the floor. The bedroom stunk! We were disgusted and told the boy's father to get a grip on his son and, until he did, he would never be allowed in our house again. We didn't let Andrew off the hook either. If this lad had not been the son of the brother that gave the lead in his meeting in Watford, I have no doubt they would both have been excommunicated.

As I look back on it now, by encouraging the older folk to drink, it should have been expected that the younger ones would follow suite.

Independent thinking was regarded as wrong. We were led by the Universal Leader. If our thinking differed from his, then there was something wrong with us. I can remember being told I was too strong minded. Many times my thoughts would go back to my Christian beginnings, way back to London and the camp where I first fully understood the love of Jesus, and had formed my impressions of Him through the Christian activities in which I was involved. This would lead me to compare these present times with those past experiences. My first encounters with this church, all those years ago, were very happy times. The kindness and love of the Purse family and others had helped to impress the Love of Christ on me.

I would think of the things I had gone through and how I had felt the Lord's presence at such times. I had developed my own personal link with the Lord through the pain and struggles of the past, and it was this relationship that would often govern my thinking, rather than what others told me.

Speaking out would get me into trouble, but I would eventually come to the realisation that I was wrong, and the church were right and if I wanted to follow the Lord, I would have to be subject to the Universal Leader through whom the Lord spoke. We had been taught that we were the church and there was no other gathering the Lord was working with. I agreed with all this wholeheartedly, and came to believe that my independent thinking was all wrong, and I was to submit to the man God was using.

Because we regarded ourselves to be the only ones that held the truth, we were never allowed to read any other ministry but our own, and to keep up with what the Lord was saying currently, we would have to read the little *white book* each week. Well, as a mother with five children and so much entertaining to do, I would struggle to get through it, and when I did, I would feel God was pleased with me, but rather than being fed by it, it left me with a feeling of self-righteousness.

As I look back now, I feel that reading the Bible should have been my priority, others may have had the time to read both, or perhaps I should have made the time.

There were many things we could be excommunicated for besides those already mentioned, just to name a few more: swimming in public places, water sports, attending football matches, smoking and, of course, eating or drinking with those who were not one of us. Not mixing with the world was the key discipline, it was said that even sharing the driveway or a drainage system with your neighbour, was wrong and those who lived in semi-detached houses, had to look for detached houses if at all possible.

Whenever you were linked with the world you were contaminated. "Come out from among them and be ye separate says the Lord."

It was stressed that God wanted a pure assembly, untouched or influenced by the world: a clean place, where the Lord could come among us. We were the only gathering in the whole of Christendom that Christ could come to.

I have since realised there is more evil in my heart than has ever come to light on the outside. Real-worldliness is within, and what comes to light stems only from what is already within us. The things God hates most are in my heart: malice, hatred, self-righteousness, pride, vindictiveness, lover of self, you could go on... These are the things we should be judging in ourselves, things that were never in the heart of Christ. How can it be possible to achieve a clean place for the Lord while we harbour such things in our hearts? The Bible tells us: "Man looks on the outward appearance but God looks at the heart." Although I work towards righteousness, I can never fully achieve it. How thankful I am that Christ is my righteousness.

Rules and Demands Increase

Well, as time went on, more and more demands were made of us.

Men had to shave off their beards and facial hair because this was regarded as being vain. Women had to stop wearing hats, as there was too much money being spent on them and they were just a fashion item, so a simple scarf was to be worn as a head covering. I had to agree that some of the hats worn were beyond a joke, and a simple covering was all that was needed.

A casual look was required, so men had to stop wearing ties and suits, and open neck shirts had to be worn instead. There were many more restrictions that developed over the years but not much point listing them I need only to focus on the rules that affected our family.

Andrew had his first leg operation at the age of thirteen. It was then they found out he was allergic to a drug Scoline. This is administered by injection when they put you to sleep, only it did not put him to sleep, instead it seized up every muscle in his body leaving him unable to tell anyone he was not asleep. He could not move or speak and as the surgeon took hold of his leg, he (Andrew) thought they were going to operate on him while he was still awake. His chest muscles were stopping him from breathing and he felt he would suffocate, it was not until they administered the ether that he felt air being pumped into his lungs again and he knew no more until he awoke.

That experience proved to be a really frightening experience, leaving behind months of mental trauma, Andrew would call us during the night thinking it was all happening again and we would have to reassure him. Then *hell* seemed to be always worrying him and he would continually say that God did not love him. It took him a long time to recover from this experience.

All the children did well at school, except Andrew. We had been told that his concentration would have been affected as a result of the heart stoppage. Although the other children did well enough to go to university, our church children were not allowed to go because of the worldly influences and activities that took place at university. Things that were regarded as unfit for children. They did, however, seem to do just as well by leaving school and going straight into employment.

There is so much about Andrew in this account but, as you read on, I am sure you will understand why. Please don't think, as result of his troubles, that he was quiet and subdued in fact as he grew older he was the opposite, the life and soul of any party, always playing pranks on people, anything for excitement and fun.

I can remember we had a brother in the church that used to roll his R's, Andrew phoned him one evening and told him he was from BT and was checking his phone line and would he say the word, Rhubarb.

The brother obliged, "Rhubarb", he said, rolling his R.

Andrew said he could not hear him, so that brother repeated, "Rhubarb, Rhubarb, Rhubarb."

Andrew thanked him and put the phone down. He related what he had done to some of the lads in the church so that when we had our next meeting these lads were waiting outside the entrance for this brother to turn up and as he did so they all shouted

"Rhubarb Rhubarb Rhubarb", rolling their R's as they said it.

The brother was furious, and after the meeting, had those all lined up for a good ticking off. There were many more occasions similar to that. The other four children were so different in character, quieter and more reserved, never causing any trouble or concern.

Beth and Luke both developed asthma. Luke was admitted to hospital twelve times but it was never as severe as Andrew had been. We were able to keep Beth at home but we had to be careful with her as too much exertion would set her asthma off.

Luke was a good runner, coming second in the county. On one occasion he was having difficulty breathing just before a race and didn't think he could do it, so he prayed and, by the time he stood up to run, his prayer had been answered. Our second and third born were free of the complaint but asthma has always been something of a burden in our household since Andrew introduced it, and now we see it passing on to our grandchildren.

The third operation on Andrew was when he was seventeen. He was put in a ward with adult men. As you can imagine, having been bought up in our church, he had led a sheltered life, now here he was, open to all sorts of what we would call worldliness, giving him a taste of what there was to be had. He came out of hospital after three weeks, a changed person. He was going places and doing things without our knowledge. We hoped it would pass, as I suppose parent's do in those teenage years. All our children respected us, and even at this time, Andrew did treat us with respect but was not as open as to what he was getting up to. I expect he knew the trouble we would all be in if he were found out.

All the children did well at school, except Andrew. We had been told that his concentration would have been affected as a result of the heart stoppage. Although the other children did well enough to go to university, our church children were not allowed to go because of the worldly influences and activities that took place at university. Things that were regarded as unfit for children. They did, however, seem to do just as well by leaving school and going straight into employment.

Separation and Excommunication

This chapter has been the hardest one to write for what happened next devastated the whole family, and nothing else compares to the heartache and sorrow it brought about.

As I explained earlier, there are two kinds of assembly discipline. One is to be excommunicated. You could be excommunicated for all sorts of reasons and nothing was to be covered up.

The other kind of disciplinary action was to be shut up. If you are to be shut up, you are not excommunicated but you are not allowed to attend any of the services and no one is allowed to contact you apart from two members of the leadership team who are called priests. They are sent to see if you are fit to be restored or released. This would often happen if you had someone living with you who had done something wrong and was under investigation, and then your house would be regarded as unclean as long as that person was living in your house, all this is taken from the book of Leviticus.

As a family, we obeyed this to the letter, keeping separate from the world and endeavouring to keep all that was demanded of us. I understand now that human effort and man's demands lead only to self-righteousness, breakdown and failure. How important it is to follow Christ and wait for Him to convict us, acting on his guidance and not rules.

We are not all at the same stage in our individual Christian walk and to be bundled into one pen, as it were, all doing the same thing, at the same time, in the same way, even if we do not believe or understand the reason, leads to confusion. God leads us as individuals, step by step, and does not overwhelm us or put burdens on us that are too heavy to be borne. Our walk with Christ is motivated by love and not by rules.

As a result of their rules and regulations, many members fail to keep true to the doctrine of separation and John was one of them. Although he confessed his failure to the leadership, asking for help to overcome failure, he was excommunicated because (according to them) the assembly needs to be cleared of any wrongdoing, no matter how much the person repents or needs help and restoration. If the wrongdoer had any chance of coming back to the fold, they were expected to leave home until such time the church felt God had forgiven them. In other words, they were "Put outside the camp until the sore had been healed" as would happen to children of Israel in the Old Testament.

The idea was that the person was to be left alone with God, with no visits or communication with anyone in the Fellowship. This is not only based on the Old Testament but also on 1 Corinthians 5:13: "Expel the immoral brother from among you."

After about three months, two members of the leadership, known as the priests, would visit and they would report their findings to the Universal Leader who at that time lived in Canada. To make things even more uncertain in our case, was the fact that one of the priests visiting John had had a business dispute with him some months before. In fact, while all this was going on he would approach John's retail customers and encouraged them to buy his speciality cakes and biscuits which were very similar, if not the same, as John's. So I really did not have the confidence in this person being given the role of priest in our case.

As I've said, once you have been excommunicated, you had to leave the family home, and so it was that John who confessed to some worldly activity was regarded unfit for the fellowship and was excommunicated and had to leave the family home, leaving me alone with five children, little knowing that it would be nearly four years before we were together again.

That first night away from home, I understand John slept in his van in a service station, then for the next few nights he slept in his warehouse. Eventually he bought a touring caravan to live in. I was not allowed to talk to him or even acknowledge him in the street if I were to see him. I was told I had to cut him off completely and leave him alone with God.

During those four years I was extremely anxious, bearing in mind the business dispute there had been between John and the elder dealing with his case.

Life only got worse. Andrew was now eighteen and had to have another operation on his leg, spending another three weeks in hospital. Of course John was not allowed to see him, or even know he was there.

That night, after the operation, the doctor was called up to the ward in an emergency. Andrew was in trouble with his heart. (He was born with a faulty heart valve) The whole three weeks he was in hospital he kept vomiting; the medical staff were puzzled as to why this was.

The first morning after he had arrived home from hospital, I took his breakfast up to him and found him crying. You never saw Andrew cry. He was pretty tough when it came to suffering, so to see him crying, I knew there must be something drastically wrong. I asked him if his leg was hurting, his answer was, "I can't tell you mum, you have been so good to me."

I encouraged him to tell me so that I could help him. He eventually opened up and told me of something he had done three months earlier, but had stopped, not wanting to continue with it, but because he had not confessed, it was still laying on his conscience. His words to me were: "That night in hospital, when I was so ill, I thought I was dying and going to hell, and the fear kept making me vomit."

My heart sank. While I was glad he felt able to talk to me about it, I knew what was coming. He asked me to go and tell the leadership, I didn't want to do it, I had already lost John but Andrew insisted he wanted to be free and forgiven, and I knew I would be in trouble if I encouraged him not to say anything. As he could not put his leg to the floor for the next three months, it was left for me to go down stairs and make the phone call.

I phoned one of the leaders to tell them that Andrew wanted to see them. Two members came around that same evening and spoke to Andrew. I was not with them so didn't know what was said, but they came to me after seeing him and told me he was to be excommunicated and he was to leave the home. I reminded them that he had just come out of hospital and could not put his foot to the floor for three months. In that case they told me he would have to remain at home until the plaster on his leg had been removed, and I too would have to be shut up, as the house would be unclean while Andrew was living in it. So I was not allowed to any of the services as long as Andrew was in the house with me.

In the light of all this, our eldest daughter who was now fifteen and our second son who was thirteen and my mother who lived in the granny-flat that had been built for her, all had to leave and move in with other members of the church so that they would not be contaminated and could continue going to the services and be free to meet with other members of the Fellowship.. Beth and Luke, being only six and five, were too young to leave me, so they were not allowed out to the services either.

I was left with the following instructions:

First I was not to eat with Andrew. I was to keep separate and, to do this, I was told Andrew must remain in his bedroom, have all his meals in there and was not to have access to any other part of the house Beth and Luke were not to go into Andrew's room.

I knew from the start it would be impossible to keep all these regulations and, knowing Andrew's personality, it would be cruel to keep him holed up in one room, so I told him he could have the run of the house and I, with Beth and Luke would live in the granny-flat.

From that moment on I kept a diary so that, when John came back, we could share our experiences with each other.

The following are extracts from that diary, perhaps a bit disjointed, as they were never intended to be made public.

April 2nd	Cried on and off most of the night, could hear Andrew crying too, it's like a bad dream I can't escape from it, try to pray, can't get through, why is there no answer? Read my Bible, didn't help. Felt sick all day. Wanted to comfort Andy but I must not, got to stay strong for the family or will never get back together again.
April 3rd	Another bad night, nights are the worst. Heard Andy crying. Wonder who my children are staying with, I wish they would tell me. Must stand firm; the whole families depending on me to do the right thing.
April 8th	Andrew asked me today if there was any hope for what he had done. I said "It's between you and God". I wanted so badly to say yes there was hope, the boy needs help, he needs hope but I've been told he has to be left alone with God.
April 13th	Beth and Luke are fretting for the others. I took them to the park after school. Over a week now, no one's been in touch. I heard Andrew crying again last night, can't go into him, got to do the right thing or God will not help. O God this is so hard.

April 18th   I am so thankful that Andrew came to me today quoting the prodigal son who devoured his goods with harlots. "Yet the father ran to meet him" he said, Andy has made a move in the right direction, why is the Father not running to meet him?

Although I feel so relieved that he has come to the fact he can be forgiven."Of course there is forgiveness", I told him.

"but when?" he asked.

I wish I could tell him.

April 21st   It's been three weeks now and no one has been to see him. He's getting desperate says he feels like a bird in a tiny cage looking for the door but there isn't one. My heart aches for him. The leaders don't have to live with this situation they lay the law down and walk away. I'm worrying about John. Wonder where he's gone.

April 22nd   Can't keep the children away from Andrew it's just impossible, why should the children suffer? I am worried about John, where is he living? Has anyone been to see him yet? If I could see the end of all this I could keep going, it's just the not knowing that is getting to me.

April 24th   Took the children fishing at Hemel today and took Andrew with me, was that wrong? Just had to get him out of the house, it is all so cruel and unnatural. I'm sure I'm not doing wrong.

April 25th   Worried about John most of the night - will he give up?

Andrew's just told me there are other things he has done wrong and did he need to confess them too? Because he did not want to come back into fellowship and find he had to face other things he had done. I asked him what sort of things? When he told me what they were I feel they were not that bad and I've told him that I think the greater thing would cover the lesser and have not encouraged him to do any more confessing, it would only prolong the dreadful situation we are in.

April 26th   They have still not been to see him. Took him for a ride in the car, we went to Hemel by the river again, cheered Beth and Luke up a bit, they need their friends to play with. It is so hard to keep going. I wonder if they've been to see John.

Oh for goodness sake! Why do they treat me like this? Why don't they tell me what is happening and where are my other children and where is John? Why am I left like this when I'm trying to do the right thing? What's the use of praying? God's not there.

April 29th   Andy still seems to be troubled about his past, he insists on me phoning the leaders and telling them he wants to see them to confess the other things that are on his mind. I'm going to have to do it; he is so troubled.----------- I wished I hadn't rung.

They said, "We have no desire to see him at present."

How can they be so indifferent?

How can I relate that to Andy? I dare not tell him.

May 2nd   Not feeling well today and having to think of things to do with Beth and Luke to keep them happy it is so difficult they have no friends to play with. Andy's getting pins and needles in his leg. He says it drives him mad at night, could it be the feeling coming back?

May 3rd   Andy asked me today if I had phoned and had they [the leadership] said when they were coming to see him. I had to tell him what they had said. He broke down and cried saying: "I can't go on, I'm giving up." He took his crutches and went out. I asked where he was going but he didn't answer, I am worried, I couldn't follow him as I had Beth and Luke.

Andy came home four hours later but wouldn't tell me where he had been.

God, I'm trying to find you in all this.

May 4th   Saw my friend June today while shopping, she waved and smiled at me, made me feel happier just a little bit of contact with someone I knew, just to be acknowledged lifted my spirits today.

May 6th   The leader phoned me today they were coming to see me on Thursday but not Andy. For goodness sake, they don't need to see me, it's Andy they should be seeing, and I know he will feel dreadful when I tell him they are coming to the house but will not be seeing him. I just wish they were not coming at all.

May 8th   Yes, it's Thursday. The priests have just left, didn't get much out of the visit, and feel more depressed now than before they came. Asked if I was keeping separate from Andrew, was I eating with him? Was I keeping the children away from him? Told them keeping the children away was impossible they run everywhere.

I can't believe this: I told them that while shopping I had seen my friend June and how glad I was that she had smiled and waved, they responded as follows, "Who gave her permission to wave to you?" And turning to the other said, "Did you?"

"No" replied the other he hadn't. I feel like a criminal after all what had I done wrong? Shouldn't they be encouraging and supporting me I'm trying to do the right thing. Is all this coming from The Universal Leader or is it just these priests taking this hard-line?

Continual crying gives me eye infections. Asked them about John, they told me I didn't need to know. John, what is happening to you? Are you still hanging on and are you as miserable as me?

May 18th 10 days since I entered anything in this diary simply because it would be the same old story struggling to get through every day and every night.

May 22nd They came to see me again today it's two weeks since their last visit. Same questions asked about keeping separate. Told them next door was complaining about the fence at the bottom of the garden, had hoped they would send someone from the congregation to help fix it but no, just told me how to do it.

Neighbours both sides have noticed some of the family are missing. This is making me feel embarrassed. How could anyone explain?

May 28th The children and I have stopped living in grandma's flat. I'm using my common sense, I feel resentful they don't care so why should I, I'll do for my children or what is left of them what I think right for them.

May 29th They came to see Andy today, first time in nearly 2 months. How excited he was, I think he thought they were going to have him back in the Fellowship. Wouldn't that have been great, (Wishful thinking) no, they had heard from John G (a schoolboy in the Fellowship) that a girl in his class, an old friend of Andy's had met up with him in the park and he had kissed her.

I was not allowed to be in the room when they visited him. Andy told me they sat in silence for some time neither side saying anything, he felt embarrassed and didn't know what to say, eventually one of the priests asked if he had been behaving himself. When he said he had, they then bought up this incident. Andrew admitted that he had met up with this girl one afternoon in the park. As he had not related this incidence to them himself they still regard him as unfit for Christian fellowship.

What a disappointment, we had waited two months for this visit, how much longer must we live like this? Andrew has just confessed to me it was the afternoon he stormed out because they wouldn't see him that he'd met this girl in the park.

They've not given me any news of my other children or my mum; don't know where they are staying. I'm trying to cheer Andrew up but feel so depressed myself.

June 1st	The three months are up and Andy has to go to Stanmore tomorrow to have his plaster off. Just phoned one of the priests to tell him I shall have to go with him and someone will have to have the children, but have been told there was no need for me to go, I am just to drop him off at the station. I tried to explain he had not put his foot to the floor for three months and he will find it difficult to walk but he insisted I do what he says. I don't agree with him as a mother, how can I? Why must they add to all his suffering? How can they do this to him? I'm up against a brick wall, if I don't do what they say we will never get the family back together
June 2nd	The surgeon was very surprised he had gone up alone. Andy said coming home the train was full and he had to stand with just his crutches to lean on. When I met him at the station, I could see he was in a lot of pain. Why did I let them do this to him? If I cross them, that's the end.

His leg was badly swollen and burning hot, had to keep putting cold compresses on it hope no damage has been done.

June 9th	It's a week now since his plaster has been off, still swelling up and painful, keeps him awake at night. One of the priests phoned me today to say that now his plaster was off he would have to leave home. I said, "He can't, he's still in pain and finding it difficult to walk as yet."

Now I'm in trouble; I argued with him [the priest] over the phone and told him that what he was suggesting was inhuman. "Whose authority are you under?" I asked.

"The Universal Leaders", I was told and, "while Andrew is in the house, the rest of your family will not be allowed home and you will not be allowed out to the meetings." He continued by saying that I had to tell him [Andrew] tonight that he had to leave home. I told him I was not letting him go until his leg was strong enough. "Well", he said, "you know the consequences."

June 10th   Couldn't bring myself to tell Andy last night got to tell him this morning. Andrew wept, he has asked me what else he could do to be forgiven and where could he go. I had no idea so rang one of the priests and asked where was Andrew to go. His reply: "You don't tell someone withdrawn from where to go".

June 11th   One of the priests came on his own to see me this morning. I was surprised to see him without the other as they always come in twos He has just told me that in the beginning I was originally shut up because Andrew was in the house but after arguing with him the other day I was now shut up because of my own insubordination.

I'm shaking like a leaf, I feel sick, I'm trapped, seems they can do what they like with me and there is no way out and no one to tell what is going on, nothing makes sense, Has it ever? Who is there to talk to? no one will take any notice of me in the position I'm in.

The priests will just give the church members their side of the story. What are they doing to Andy? hasn't he been punished enough? How are they treating John? Are they treating him like they are treating us? What are they telling the members about me? I don't trust them now.

June 12th   Andy left today he found his dad was living in a caravan in Stopsley and has gone to live with him. I tried to tell him before he went not to give up, it was heartbreaking. Well at least John will have company now.

Now I'm on my own with Beth and Luke and still unable to go to the meetings because of my insubordination. I try to pray but too agitated, my prayers don't go anywhere, I read my Bible, I can't take it in, too troubled.

June 14th	Missing everyone so much. Beth and Luke have each other but it is so hard for them, they have lost their other brother now and keep asking when they can go back to the meetings, but for me they would be back in the Fellowship now Andy has gone.

    I'm trying to sort myself out but I can't I just can't get to the bottom of it all. Where is God? I call, He does not answer. I can't find him. I'm in a dark place so dark I can't see my way out.

    I worry about Andy then I worry about John, can't worry about both at once. Will I ever see them again? Will we ever be a family again?

June 16	A strange thing happened today went to the Arndale [mall] and seemed to get lost, didn't recognise any of the shops, couldn't place together where I was, so sat on a seat to see if I could work it all out, a lady next to me asked if I was all right. Little did she know, I told her "I could not think where I was."

    "You're in the Arndale love, are you sure you're all right?"

    After resting it all came back. This has never happened to me before, bit worrying, am I going mad?

June 17th	Today's been a bad day. If only I could stop worrying, I'd probably find God in all this, sometimes I think I've found Him and then I lose Him again. Trouble is there is no one to talk to or share my thoughts with Beth and Luke are too young they ask continually when they're going to see their brothers and sister, how can I explain all this to them? In prison you get company, in my prison I get none. There are no windows in mine, I'm closed in, and there is no air to breathe.
June 20th	Had another memory loss today, this time outside the house had to stand by a wall to work out where I was. It's odd.
June 21st	Wondering now if I've been withdrawn from as no one has contacted me since last priest came round, am I still shut up or have I been excommunicated? I wonder would they let me know, this is wearing me down, if only someone could tell me when it would end I could live through it, I'd endure it if I could see a light at the end of the tunnel. How long do I have to live like this? I read my Bible to find an answer but there isn't one.

June 22nd   Went to the doctor's today about memory loss and headaches. He told me he thought that the tension in my neck muscles are causing the headaches and restricting the flow of blood to the brain. Asked me what I was tensed up about, couldn't tell him the truth, he'd never understand, said it was family problems. Asked me if I was eating well, sent me for a blood test and gave me sleeping tablets.

June 25th   The Priests came round late this evening. I asked if I had been withdrawn from, their reply: "What makes you think that?" I reminded them of what the other priest had said to me that I was shut up because of my insubordination and since I had not been released after Andrew left I thought, perhaps I had been withdrawn from. I asked if I could come back to the meetings and join the fellowship again. They told me I could not do this until I had severed all my links with John. That involves getting a legal separation, getting the house put into my name, and giving the car back to John because that was in his name too.

I'm devastated, why have they only just told me all this? Why didn't they explain all this when John first left home? I could've been sorting these things out weeks ago. How long will this take? Beth and Luke need the company of others.

Beth was still awake when they left, came downstairs caught me crying, asked me why and then asked if they said we could go back to the meetings. "Not yet" I said.

June 28th   Went to see a solicitor this morning for a legal separation, broke down and cried in his office, told him I really did not want to do this, but got through it.

June 29th   Yesterday I did the legal separation bit, today tried to get the house put into my name, told I need John's cooperation. The priests will have to go and see John, how long will that take?

Tonight, I sat on the end of my bed with a bottle of codeine tablets and an overwhelming desire to be released, to find a way out of the darkness, I can't describe, it presses down and it surround me, I don't want carry on. I cannot go on feeling the way I do. I took the top off the bottle wondering would it be painless. I stood up, bent down and looked at Beth and Luke who were sleeping in my bed, and that brought me to my senses. How selfish I was, it was all about me. How could I be thinking like this? they needed me, they were in this with me. "Lord, help me", I cried aloud.

That was the last entry I made in my diary.

I have since heard of several other members who have been in a position similar to this who have taken their own lives. One young fellow had been excommunicated because his wife had found cigarettes under his pillow; he was withdrawn from and eventually threw himself under a train. Another hung himself. Another bulldozed his house down with his wife and children still in it. You have to be in that situation to understand the torment that both partners feel.

As time went on I was falling in and out of depression, even doubting if God really existed. He was not answering me. Was I going through all this and God did not exist?

He was always on my mind, whether it was doubts of his existence or requests to Him for fresh manifestations of his presence or pleads for Him to restore our family.

I wrote the following verses on one such occasion, they sum up how I felt:

I stand in the valley, the Valley of tears.
Calling you God the ancient of years,
You say I'm your child and it's all for my good.
And all in your presence will be understood.
Reflecting life's sorrows one day will I see.
This road that I tread was the best one for me.

I want to hold on but my faith is so weak.
I'm calling you now, it's your presence I seek.
When Satan infers that you may not exist.
You know I am tempted to listen to this.
Forgive my unfaithfulness, help me hold fast.
O God of my future, on thee I am cast.

Bring joy in my darkness, bring peace in my pain.
Show me your presence, come closer again.
When I search through your Book let me see you appear,
Will you hold me and keep me and prove you are near,
Just a touch of your hand, or a Word from your throne,

That I'm wrapped in your arms and I don't walk alone.

My Shepherd my saviour, my guide and my God.
Help me bend to your will, your staff and your rod.
Help me to find as I peer through the dark.
A sense of your presence to comfort my heart.
Knowing you're there and you're still at my side.
Your peace overcoming the hurt that's inside.

Help me to trust you, to trust in your love.
To feel that you're near, not remote far above.
Though waters are raging they will not consume.
Through waves and through billows please see I reach home.
Show me your promises trusted and sure.
To hold me and keep me and help me endure,

Help me to praise in the height of the storm.
Though mingled with sadness let joy be reborn.
Let me walk in the valley accepting your will.
Knowing you love me and walk with me still.
Help me remember each crisis in life.
Your presence, Lord Jesus, will always suffice.

My Search for the Truth

Several weeks later and I was still waiting to hear from the solicitor who is transferring the house into my name, all the other transfers had by now been done but the house seemed to take so much longer.

When I finally got confirmation that this had been completed, I phoned one of the priests to let him know that all they had asked of me had now been completed and could I now be released, have my children back and attend the meetings again? He told me that I was in too much of a hurry and would have to wait until my matters had been discussed in the assembly. I remember thinking at that point that they did not want me back or that they just didn't care, they had no compassion and saw no urgency in releasing or setting me free.

The day I was released happened also to be our second son Peter's birthday. He, along with our daughter Sarah and my mother, were all able to come back home. He told me that his coming home was the best birthday present he could have had. I cannot explain the relief it was to have them back and to be able to celebrate his birthday together. Luke and Beth were so excited the house seemed alive again, but there were still two empty spaces, we could not forget that my John and Andy were not there.

The whole family had suffered in so many different ways yet still, I could not see that the ministry and the Universal Leader were wrong. I thought, at that time, it was just our local church and it had all been a result of the ignorance of the two priests that did not handle us in the right way.

Not long after being released and back in my church again, I had several operations on my damaged hand; I think it was five in all, all at the orthopaedic hospital in London. On one occasion, something so significant happened. Someone kept asking the Sisters of my ward to ask me if I knew of someone named Barbara. I said, "Yes, I know a lady from Watford with that name."

The Sister said, "Well, this woman thinks she knows you." She asked, "Shall I send her up?"

"You can do" I said

As she came through the door of my ward, I shook my head. "No, I do not know her." I said.

Then I heard this woman say: "It is, it is, it's my sister!"

As she came nearer, I began to recognise her. I couldn't believe it, it had been thirty-four years since I had last seen her and even the name, Barbara, hadn't connected this woman to the sister I had lost all those years ago. After all that had happened since I had last seen her, my memory and concern for her had faded. Even her name had not rung any bell when the ward sister had asked me if I knew a Barbara. I could only recall the one I knew in Watford.

It turned out that Barbara was a chef in the hospital kitchen and she had seen my meal menu with the name Wendy on it and had enquired as to the reason for my being admitted. Then, having been told I was in for a hand op, she wanted to find out if it was, indeed, her sister.

I was still in my church then and she had been excommunicated thirty-four years ago, but with the excitement of seeing her again, and as she had been out of the fellowship for so long, I made that an excuse for mixing with her again. We had so much to catch up on and, as I was in that hospital for three weeks, on that occasion, we had lots of opportunities to do just that. She would come and visit me after her shift was over.

After several conversations, I realised I would never have found her if I had been looking for her. She had divorced Frank, who she had taken Mother to court to marry and had re-married so her name had changed. When I had last seen her, she was living in Leicester, now she was living in London. I couldn't understand why the Lord had bought her to me like this. I knew there had to be a reason.

When I left the hospital, I knew I may never be able to see her again but I took down her address.

Of course, I knew, when I got home, I would have to confess to the time I had spent with her. Mother was really interested to know all about her.

As Barbara had been out of the fellowship for so long, and the fact that I happened to be in the same hospital, allowed me to be forgiven for the contact I had with her, but I was told never to contact her again unless she was interested in repenting and returning to the fellowship.

After the excitement of seeing Barbara and having Sarah and Peter and mum back with me again, the months wore on. It was becoming harder and harder to accept that John and Andy was still not with us. I had learnt by this time that John was living in a caravan in Luton but was never quite sure where Andy was, as he had left his father.

It was difficult trying to keep the four children happy while bearing these concerns for the other two, knowing they were out there somewhere. We were given very little news of them and, if they had tried to contact us, there would have been even less hope of them coming back.

As the months went into years, I wondered if they would ever come home again, it was eating away at me. I knew if I were to object or disobey, I would lose the rest of the family and be back in what the church calls the 'shut up' situation. I just couldn't go through that again, so it was best to be submissive. I thought if I was submissive toward the leaders, God would come in, eventually, and complete the family again.

As I've said before, God was always on my mind. I was always trying to seek His approval and trying to feel His presence. I knew, through my other experiences in the past, how I would know that He was with me, but throughout the whole of this experience I struggled to find Him at all, apart from on a very few occasions now and then.

Looking back now I realize if I had found Him in all this conflict, I would have been content and would not be where I am today. I understand now that God was leading me to freedom, where Love rules and not legality. Oh! How I long that my two children Sarah and Peter could or would see the beauty and joy of the freedom God gives us in Christ.

In my search for God, I began making the Bible my primary source of authority rather than the *White Book*. The book of Isaiah was where I began to find Him. I began reading chapter by chapter, then going over them all again, because here I was seeing a different God to the God I knew. The God I knew was hard, legal and demanding, yet the God of Isaiah I found, is forgiving and compassionate, pronouncing judgement, yet giving His people a way to escape from the judgement they (and we) deserve. He did not want to continue to have to punish the Israelites (nor us), in fact, He endured the punishment we should suffer, so that we could go free and have a happy relationship with Him, a relationship which He so much desires to have with us.

Isaiah writes: "He [God] was wounded for my transgressions; He was bruised for my iniquities..." (Isaiah 53:4-5)

Why should my church not show the same compassion? I began to compare the God Isaiah writes about to the God I thought I knew, and I began to realise that my understanding of the nature of God did not correspond with that of Isaiah's. I suppose the responsibility of having neglected the Bible for the *White Book* was mine but we relied so much on the Universal Leader's Ministry, his rules and his interpretation of Scripture, that we did not think for ourselves, we just accepted without question. In fact, we were led to believe that it was far more important to read the *White Book* rather than finding time to read the Bible. A new *Book* would come out every week so, by the time you had finished one, you would have to be ready for the next so as to keep up with what the Lord was saying through our leader. It was a struggle to read anything else for by the time you had looked after your children and coped with the large amount of entertainment you had to do, it was as much as one could do to read the entire booklet in a week let alone the Bible which, for my part, was being neglected. We did have Bible studies in the services but gradually these Bible readings grew to focus more and more on the Universal Leader. So in my search to find God, I had to lay aside the *White Book* and make the Bible my priority. It was then that I began to see the true character of God, not other people's idea of Him. That hard and unforgiving spirit did not represent the God found in Isaiah.

A light began to dawn, questions arose in my mind; I would turn them away as sinful thoughts. Such thoughts or ideas would bring me into trouble again if I was to voice them.

While this was going on, I was still getting visits and reprimands from the local priests. On one occasion they came to see me because someone had told them I had a family photo on the wall and that my husband and Andrew were in it, so they came to tell me that, on that account, I had to take it down. On another occasion, I was visited after I had arranged an 18th birthday party for my son and I was told by them to cancel it. The priests informed me I was making special friendships and special friendship was not allowed. Another occasion I had let our son buy a small motorbike so he could get to work, the ministry stipulated no motorbikes. I never once remember a visit of encouragement, it was always a visit to reprimand me and, usually, I would end up in tears.

Years rolled by yet there was still no news of Andy or John ever coming back to join the family. They were not allowed to get in touch with us or we with them, and what little news we did get, came only from the priests who would visit them maybe once in every four months, but would relay very little or nothing to me of their visits.

Then one day I received a letter from Andrew. Here are a few quotes from it:

Dear mum,

I have done all I can to try and come back but I can't make it, I try to do what's right, I can last a month without doing anything wrong and then I slip up and I have to tell them when they come to see me. I have even smashed up my television hoping they would see I was serious in trying to do the right thing, I have kept myself separate but nothing I do is good enough. I love you so much and just want to come home, my heart breaks, thank you for all you have done and I'm sorry for all the trouble I have caused you, I will love you always,

Andy.

My heart was breaking too. How could they expect a young lad to be so righteous in every detail with no Christian support? It was hard to make sense of it all. My head was becoming full of contradictory questions, was it me that was wrong or this church with its unreasonable rules.

I was sitting in one of the services one time and I looked around at the approximately 400 members who met together from the surrounding areas and I remember asking myself, "Is it me that is wrong? How can I be right when all these people think they are right? Why should I have different views about the assembly than all these people here? How can I be right and all these wrong?"

On the 25th of April 82 I received this second letter from Andrew:

Dear Mum,

I must write. I feel so confused, although I do not want to hurt you, because I love you, mum, so much. I would love to come home and see you. It has been nearly four years now so much has happened. I badly want to come back but I keep slipping up, only I suppose in little things, but it takes me back to square one again. It has all become unbearable. I have tried... honest.

Now I have fallen in love with someone. In all this time away from the family, I suppose I have been looking for affection. No one can understand, unless they have been in the same situation I have been in, just how boring it is. There were times when I went for ages refusing everything that would prevent me coming home again. I would often speak to Jesus. I know if they had had me back, I would never do anything like that again and the church's company would have helped me. The brothers would come and see me and then go and, as they left, I would know it would be a long time before they would come again. Most of the times I slipped up, were when I got tipsy on cider trying to cheer myself up and, afterwards, I would be in despair because I knew I would have to tell them. I could not come back on false pretences.

So as you can see, it seems so impossible, it has torn me apart, it has been absolute hell. Sorry this letter has been so depressing but it can't be avoided. Please could you send me some photos of you and the others and tell me about everyone. I really miss you all, it is so hard. Give my love to everyone and try to keep your pecker up. It is so cruel that dad should be out for so long. It's terrible to see him on his own all this time even though he has been keeping himself. I am longing to see you together again.

All my love

Andy

Some months later, I received a letter from John.

Dearest Wendy,

It is many years since I had anything to do with you, nearly four now, a very long time to be without my dear wife and family. I don't know of any Scripture that supports husbands leaving wives, in fact, Scripture says, "What God has joined together, let no man put asunder."

I have never been impressed with priestly visits. I still love you all but, under the circumstances, I cannot go on day after day and year after year just looking into space, it is driving me insane. I have done everything possible to get back.

What's the use of preaching the gospel and saying, "no penalty", and then keeping someone out of the fellowship for years. I have taken as much as I can stand now, if you care to contact me at the above or phone, I would be only too pleased. One of the things that upset me most was, when Andrew asked for a Bible, as he had lost his, the priest said he would normally give his own Bible but he just couldn't give it to Andrew.

There are many more things I could mention going back over the years but what's the use? It will only upset you, I just feel now it is best to be out of it all, remaining causes sorrow after sorrow, I am sure the Lord does not want us to go on the way we are, I have had plenty of time to think things over, and I only hope, dear, you will come to me.

Looking forward to hearing from you as you are still my wife.

With all my love to you and all the children

John

The reference made in this letter to the Scripture "What God has joined, let no man separate", was in line with the Scripture I had read in 1 Corinthians a few evenings before. In 1 Corinthians 7:10 it reads: "To the married I [the Lord] give this command: a wife must not separate from her husband and, if she does, she must remain unmarried or else be reconciled to her husband, and the husband must not divorce his wife."

I remember I called my son Peter and told him what I had just read. He told me that, if I continued with that line, I would find myself out of fellowship. I knew by this remark that I could not share my thoughts with anyone else for fear of being *shut up* again or withdraw from. The trauma of this would be too much to take; besides, I needed more time to think. I was not yet sure, at that point, what that Scripture really meant, but John's letter and the understanding of the Scripture he had reminded me of, added to the doubts I already had. I began to really doubt my position, as separated from my husband, as being right. Besides, if it was wrong to be separated, how would I deal with it? Were the church right? Did God want me to remain separated from my husband? I prayed that God would show me. One thing I did know was that the harsh treatment I was receiving was not the spirit of Christ. Nor was the unforgiving spirit that was being extended to both Andrew and John, displaying the God of the Bible.

Our son, Peter was now eighteen, Sarah was twenty-one, Beth was nine and

Luke was seven. I loved them all dearly, they were the major part of my life, so were John and Andrew, it was like tearing myself apart. Whichever way I looked, there was sorrow. I felt as I did on other occasions, banging my head against a brick wall with no escape. It was the same feeling I had when John's parents had left the church only it was much closer to home now. It was my children; my husband and I could now feel more deeply just how John's mother must have felt.

I could not eat or sleep and was losing weight. I had no, energy to look after the house or to arrange the entertainment we had to do so much of. My memory losses were becoming more frequent although I tried to hide it from the children, and my tears had to wait for bedtime. The decision had to be made and, whichever way I chose, it would have a devastating impact on all our lives.

There were times when I would look at Sarah and Peter and ask myself how I could leave them. What would happen to them if I did? What would it do to them? I knew I could keep Beth and Luke because they were too young to be taken from me, but to take them away from their older siblings, their grandma and others in the fellowship would be a dreadful thing to do. Where would it all end?

I would, at times, think back to my childhood and the contact I had with other Christians in those days before Mother introduced me to the church. I remember the joy I felt in knowing Christ for the first time.

I was happier then. Christians outside the fellowship seem to show so much more love and kindness than I ever experienced from those I fellowshipped with in Luton. I don't think I really thought at that time that the Universal Leader was wrong even though I did question his ministry concerning husbands and wives being separated. I think it was the harsh treatment I received at the hands of the so-called leaders in Luton that attributed largely to the decision I ultimately made.

Another thought that troubled me was the dispute there had been between one of the priests and John over business matters. As this priest was in the same line of business as John, and knowing he (the priest) was canvassing John's customers, led me to believe that keeping John out of the fellowship was done with an ulterior motive...who knows?

There was one noticeable event that brought about my final decision to leave. A young girl had come to stay with us because her parents had been *shut up*. During her stay, one evening we had a silly conversation about animals and I remember her remarking that animals had souls. I pointed out that I didn't think they did and that only humans had souls as Genesis tells us that we were made in the image of God and

God breathed into man the breath of life. This is not said in relation to the animals. She got quite argumentative with me, but seeing it was something not worth discussing at such length, and not wanting to carry on the conversation, I finished it.

She must then have spoken to the two priests about it because, a few days later, I had a visit from one of them, accusing me of telling the young people that animals had souls. I know now it all sounds so ridiculous, but to think they took issue with me over something so trivial made me feel I couldn't move without them finding something to accuse me of. The fact that the accusation was the opposite of what I had told the girl both hurt and bewildered me but it only encouraged me to make the decision I was trying to make. Why should I stay and be humiliated, falsely accused and treated with such hardness any longer?

While in hospital having my hand operations, I had time to read several biographies of other Christian's experiences. Among these accounts was "Tortured for His Faith" and, "Brother Andrew". I can't remember all the other titles but I found these books to have been written by men of faith who had gone through horrendous personal experiences, trusting in God through many adversities, imprisonments, tortures, beatings and starvation and yet remaining faithful, never giving in to their captives demands to denounce their faith.

Their endurance put me to shame, yet they were not among the Christians I was walking with who professed to be the only position that was right, why, I thought, are these Christians not among us? Why hadn't God led them to us? In fact, I mentioned these books I had been reading to some elderly brother in the fellowship and asked him why he thought these Christians were not with us. His reply was that I should not be reading such books. I did wonder how he could say this and how cold and unfeeling that remark was. Here we were sitting in a comfortable living room, entertaining members of the fellowship or meeting in lavish meeting rooms, while other Christians were prepared to suffer such trials.

It made me realise there were genuine Christians out there whose love for Christ was so strong, they were prepared to suffer for the sake of His Gospel and His church, and I wanted to find them, I wanted to be part of them. Was this God calling me out or was it just my own feelings?

I knew if I left the church they would say I had turned my back on the Lord and I was no longer fit for Christian Fellowship. I would be regarded worse than worldly Christians because I had known the light and turned away from it. This was said of all those who left the fellowship. How could I endure having my two children Sarah and

Peter think of me in this way? These thoughts would play on my mind so that one day I would be staying, another day I would be leaving. I began to wish that the church would withdraw from me for something bad I had done so the decision to leave was not mine to make.

After eight weeks of this turmoil, I knew I had to make a decision of some kind if only to relieve the pressure mentally. As I said, the final decision to leave came after the incident with the young girl, but how could I tell the children? They would tell the elders and I would have them coming round, and making it so much harder. My other son and daughter, Sarah and Peter, I reasoned, were safe. They had friends and they would be looked after, they were with Christians but John and Andrew were out there and needed me.

That was the only reason I could think of to justify me leaving my two children. I knew there was probably no hope of any restoration for us to be a whole family again. I had tried for so long to have the family reunited but had failed. Maybe if I had shared my thoughts with my son and daughter, Sarah and Peter they might have come out with me, but I knew how strong their belief in the church's teaching was and they would only have joined with other members of the church in persuading me to stay. I knew I would have been *shut up* again until I had repented of such thoughts, and I couldn't face the thought of being trapped in that position again.

Eventually I wrote a letter to John, telling him I wanted to see him, and pushed the letter under his warehouse door. A few days later we met for the first time in nearly four years.

We met in his warehouse. He did not seem very pleased to see me at first which I found difficult to understand, but later he told me he thought members of the church had sent me and it was some trick they were playing. It was not until I had told him of my decision to leave the church and had explained I had not been sent by them, that we embraced and he was over the moon, as they say. It was so good to see him again after so long a time, yet my heart was still breaking and I was filled with guilt at the prospect of leaving Sarah and Peter and my mother, not knowing how it would all end. Even now, it is hard to write this without getting emotional. I was still not quite sure at that time if I was doing the right thing or not, but having taken the decision, I felt some relief despite the heartbreak I was feeling and the knowledge of what I was doing to the rest of my family.

Heart Breaks and Reunions

It was several weeks after our first meeting before it became convenient to join John as Sarah developed a throat infection and there was no way I could leave her while she was still poorly. Besides, I was glad of the extra time we had together yet, in some ways, it was only making it harder and prolonging my inevitable departure. Along with the feelings of deceit and not being able to tell them I was leaving or being able to say goodbye, was the thought that every moment may be the last time we would ever be together again.

I remember so well the day I left, I took a long look at Peter and Sarah, trying to imprint them into my memory, not knowing when, or if ever, I would see them again. It was so hard, how I wished I could have been open with them and explained it all.

Peter bought me up a cup of tea before he went to work that morning; it is too painful to explain how I felt as he handed me that cup.

I packed the car that morning and I left a note for the children to say I was going back to their father and they should do what they thought was right before the Lord, and also how I longed for them to join me. It was that last visit from the priests that cemented my decision. Why should I be bullied and humiliated when, for nearly four years, I had really tried to do all the church had asked of me?

John planned to meet me in one of the parks in Luton. I had asked him previously to take me far away as I knew the church elders would come after me, so he chose the Isle of Wight for a week-long break.

It was not until we were in the car that I told Beth and Luke we were going back to daddy. Beth was very excited, she wanted to see her daddy again, but Luke was upset. He said he didn't want to leave the church. This did not help. What was I doing? Here was Luke, crying because he didn't want to leave, something I really didn't expect from him as he was always a bit of a rascal and in fact, one of the elders had warned me that, if I didn't get a grip on Luke, he would probably end up with Andrew.

Being away that first week and being with John again helped to lift the burden from my shoulders. It was so good to be united again. Beth and Luke thoroughly enjoyed the time; they had never had a holiday before, another thing the church never allowed. The pain of leaving Sarah and Peter and my mum was with me all the time. I knew they would be hurting as well and was fully aware of all the pain and upset it would have caused back home. I didn't tell them in the note I left where I was going because I was afraid the elders in the church would find me.

After a week of mixed emotions, combined with the pleasure of being with John again and tainted with feelings of guilt for those I had abandoned , we arrived back home, (John for the first time in almost four years) to find the two children and Mother, and all their belongings, were gone. Nothing remained that indicated they had ever lived there, even their photos and snaps were taken, photos that would have reminded us of their childhood and their teenage years. There was no part of them left that I could hold onto. It was so hard to take. My mother had left two parcels on the bed for Beth and Luke, no doubt she felt sorry for them.

Andrew came round that evening, making it three and a half years since the day he had left. It was an emotional time, as you can imagine, and we stayed up well into the night, going over John and Andrew's experiences along with mine, and all that had happened over the years we had been separated.

In my eyes, at that time, Andrew had become very worldly. He, like his father, had now abandoned all hope of ever returning home. Moreover, he was now courting a girl who was not a Christian, and she was expecting his baby. They later married, but to me then, it was a great shock bearing in mind of course, how separate from the world we had been taught to be, so when Andrew asked to come back home, I refused as I just felt I had to protect Beth and Luke from the world and the activities Andrew was involved in. Remember, we had always been taught that the home was to be kept a clean place and no one involved in sin should be living there.

Looking back now, I feel it was a dreadful thing to do, especially after Andrew had waited so long to come home. Maybe you find my feelings at that time, hard to understand, but for the sake of my conscience and the feelings of guilt I still felt, I still wanted to hold onto my teaching as much as possible. Remember, I had been in the fellowship for nearly forty years and it was impossible for me to throw it all away in such a short time. In fact, it took many years of searching for the truth, holding on to what was right and disregarding what was wrong or unnecessary before I was able to put this churches doctrine behind me

I continually battled to find explanations and understanding of how I thought God looked at things and I would not accept anything I didn't understand. I never want to be caught again in circumstances like those I had left. Deciphering it all seemed endless. I felt it was useless to ask for help as no one would understand all that we had been through or the reason I had such troublesome thoughts going through my head. It would have been such a relief if someone could have explained it all to me, and I didn't have to work it all out for myself. I was weary of it all, yet I had to do the right thing before God. I had to sort it all out. I had to be free of all this guilt.

I was still finding it difficult to grasp the situation I was in when Andrew's baby arrived three months later (a little girl called Christy). I still wanted to distance myself from the world and the guilt I was feeling having left my mother and other children behind. This led to the excitement of being a grandma for the first time, not being what it should have been or could have been, and when the marriage broke up a short while after Christy was born, I didn't know how to become part of Christy's life as her mother was not a Christian. I thank the Lord that she did come to faith later on. It all sounds ridiculous now. I have moved on since those days but sincerely regret the bond that was lost with Christy, our first grandchild. I have tried to explain this to her since, and I think she understands.

For the first few months after leaving the church, we felt very isolated; we did not get in touch with any of our relatives that had left the fellowship in 1961 for about six months. We were not ready then as John had kept himself separate from his relatives as well as other people during those years when we had been apart. He did not socialise or make new friends, so that he could work his way back into the church and the family. Of course, I had no friends outside the fellowship either. If I had to describe it, I would say it was like standing in the middle of a field all alone and not knowing which way to turn, afraid of going in the wrong direction. After so many years of being told what to do and how to do it, we were now alone and had to make decisions for ourselves. We had never owned a radio or TV before or watched films, listened to music, eaten in restaurants, gone to sport centres or mixed in crowded activities.

After several months, we decided to get in touch with John's brother, David. Maybe he would understand, having left the Fellowship twenty-one years earlier. I guess he was very surprised that night he received a phone call from us. He immediately invited us round to his home.

He was a boy when we last saw him, now he was a man, married to Brenda with two children, Stephen and Annie. We were not sure of the reception we would get when we first phoned him, but we had no need to fear, he was overwhelmed with joy to see us and, as we chatted with him and Brenda, we felt that he had forgiven us for those long years of separation we had put upon them. Before the evening was out, he had asked to pray with us. This really moved us because no one in our old church had ever asked or offered to pray with us, not even during all those visits I had received from the elders.

David asked us to come round again the following evening when we met John's sister and her husband and their two daughters. Next, John met his father. We definitely did not expect the greeting we received when we knocked on his door. He had been so hostile towards us for remaining in the church all those years earlier, we had been afraid to visit him for fear he was still angry. We had put off seeing him, until now, not knowing the reception we would receive. At first, he did not recognise us - twenty-one years is a long time, he'd been so angry back in those days but now all his anger had gone and he welcomed us with open arms. It is so sad that John's mother did not live to enjoy their reunion.

Now I was free to contact my sister, Barbara. Thankfully I had kept her address and now knew why the Lord had led me to that London hospital. I would never have found her had we not met then. After several meetings with her, we are glad to see that, after so many years away from the Lord she is finding her way back on the Christian path again and continues to serve the Lord in many ways to this day.

New Beginnings

John and I were finding it very difficult to find a church or spiritual home after being indoctrinated for so long against other churches. Having being taught for so long that to attend another church would be so bad as to warrant excommunication, The old church assumed to be the only true church that were right, all other gatherings, we were told, were tainted with errors, inferring that it was better to go into the world than join another church and be involved with systemic errors. For this reason, we found it very difficult to even enter another church. The guilt we inherited from all this, was still there.

John's father lent us his radio so we could listen to a Dr Magee on Trans World Radio, a Christian program on shortwave. We listened to this every morning at 9:30am and, as we listened, we could hardly believe that there was someone, outside our old church who could not only teach us, but thrill us with his message. This kept us going for some time, and then gradually, after several months, we ventured into John's sister's church. I felt a sense of guilt as I entered the door and, at the end of the service, we felt it was not for us, I can't tell you why, but it just didn't feel right.

We knew it was going to be difficult for us, in our state of mind, to find a spiritual home.

The following Sunday we attended David's church, but this was too much for us as well. Ladies were wearing trousers, something that we were always told was wrong; we had been forbidden to dress in men's clothing. There was also not a hat to be seen. Then there was this heavy music in the church, something we were not used to. In the church we had left there was no music of any kind in their services.

Would we ever find somewhere to worship?

So we carried on listening each morning to Dr Magee. I began to feel that here was a man I could trust and maybe could give me a better understanding of Christianity outside of my old church so I wrote to him in America, telling him a little of our experiences but not wanting to run my old church down at all; there were people in there I loved and what I had done in leaving them, still played on my conscience, so did not go into too much detail.

It must have been enough as he wrote back saying, "It sounds to me as if you have come from , a very closed church and what you need now is a Bible-believing church, full of happy Christians."

He suggested we wrote to Trans World Radio in London which we did, and the reply we received, recommended we try Hightown Baptist Church in Reginald Street, Luton.

We rang the church Pastor as soon as we got their letter. His wife answered and let us know that her husband was out but would we like him to pay us a visit.

"No", we said. We did not want anyone coming to visit us, not from the church anyway. We had received so many visits from our old church previous to our leaving four years earlier that the thought of another church paying us visits was certainly not what we needed just then, so we told the pastors wife that we would just come along to the church and see what they were like.

We went the following Sunday, it was the best thing we had done for a long time. The atmosphere was wonderful and there was a presence of joy and love, it was like a tonic. You could describe our time there as the filling up of an empty vessel.

John and I looked at each other after the service and said "This is it!"

After being away from any such fellowship with other Christians for so long, and seeing what we had been through, finally finding a church home meant so much to us. The pastor came and spoke to us after that morning service, but it was after the evening service that he took us into the vestry and gave us the opportunity to let him know a little of our experiences. Afterwards he prayed with us and then explained that we needed to find where the Lord wanted us to be.

"It may not be in this church", he said, "It may be another church."

I was praying and saying, "Lord, let it be this one." Both John and I felt that evening we had found our spiritual home and couldn't wait for the next service.

The church had a good mix of all ages, young and old with about a hundred children, a lot of them coming from the housing estates with no Christian background. There were many activities that Beth and Luke could be involved in which would help them to grow. It was only a small church of about eighty members, but to have a hundred children was fantastic and I felt God had guided our family there. I still had my hang ups such as ladies wearing trousers and music in the church Even flowers in the church or children acting and doing little plays to demonstrate what they had learnt in Bible school, was very difficult for me to accept, but I thought, if I'm going to enjoy what they are enjoying in this church, I am going to have to jump in at the deep end and push all my prejudices behind me, and this is just what I did.

In those early days, I would feel so guilty when I thought of the children Sarah and Peter (the two that we had left behind.) I suppose this loss was much the same as suffering bereavement; I wanted to be able to talk about them or explain to others what they were like and the different aspects of their characters but no one other than John and Andrew, Beth and Luke knew them or had ever seen them, so how could anyone else talk or comfort me about them. In fact, we had no history we could share, no one knew our past. I would hear others in the church going over past events but I could not join in. I had nothing to share; our past could only be shared within our immediate family.

We began to see the effect all this had on Beth and Luke. There had been so many comings and goings in their lives, family members leaving, others coming back, that Beth, in particular, found it difficult to get close to anyone. First she had lost her father, then her brother, Andy, then, when we left our old church she lost all her friends along with her Grandma and her brother and sister, all hurtful experiences for any one. I guess she was afraid of being hurt again.

Luke he became very insecure for a long time. He didn't want to be left alone; he would cling to Beth while he was at school. His teacher told me he was always crying and would run to Beth at play time asking her to pray for Mummy, he would not let me leave him whenever I tried to drop him off at church activities; I had to stay with him.

Someone told me I should make a man of him and just leave him on his own, but I don't think that person understood all that Luke had been through. I knew this would not have been the right thing to do, so I would stay with him. Later on, when he was a lot older, I asked him why he would not let me leave him.

He replied, "You left Sarah and Peter and I thought you would leave me too."

That really hurt, you never know what is going on in a child's mind. If only he had told me.

As time went on, I was asked if I would work with the young people in the church. At first I said no, because I just wanted to sit back and watch, I felt I had a lot to learn and I could do that better by sitting back and observing. Here I found a kind of love that I had not experienced in my old church here no one criticised other members, no one gossiped about anyone, I wanted to learn to be like they were.

The following poem I wrote on our first anniversary at the church and it captures just how I felt at that time.

Church anniversary... Is it yours as well?
Have you a story, like to mine to tell?
When first you entered here can you review,
How much this church since then has meant to you?

Though many years have passed yet still I see,
The love in here that first attracted me,
The church that meets and prays for one another
And treats you as they would a natural brother

For I remember well the day I came,
And faces still I see that I could name,
Timidly we entered, bruised and shaking,
Battered by the storm, our hearts were breaking.

Loved ones lost, no sight of restoration,
But here it was God met our devastation,
For in this church we found so great a treasure,
The love we never thought would be our measure.

It was not the sermon or the preacher's word.
But in the things unspoken that we heard,
The gentleness of Christ to us revealed,
Through those who in this church his spirit sealed.

I from religious background still recall,
In Bible teaching thought I knew it all.
But here was something I could not explain,
That I knew nothing and must learn again

Grants not that I should break this bond of peace,
Or cause through selfish means this love to cease

Oh let me no discordant note deposit,
But turned away from all divisive gossip
To keep our church in unity and love,
That demonstrates, oh God your heart above,

To guard it as a rare and priceless treasure,
Delight your heart and gives you greatest pleasure
Grant I might be to you a willing servant,
To serve you in this church more true and fervent,
A heart where in your spirit can be free,
To give that love that others gave to me.

Preserve, oh God this haven for the weary,
That I should show your love to men more clearly,
To comfort, guide and heal the broken hearted,
Continue you in the way this church first started.

Some months later, I was asked again if I would go and help in the Young People's group known as Campaigners, to replace the pastor's wife, Doreen, who was retiring. This is a uniformed movement and I agreed as long as I did not have to wear the uniform as that was another hang up I had.

So I had the pleasure of working alongside another member of the church, my friend Joyce was a great help to me in many ways and a joy to work with. I also had the privilege of realising a small talent I had for writing plays for children. I would often write sketches for my own children and then perform them when we entertained. Now I had a lot more children to work with who were always eager to earn their Entertainment Badge.

Joyce and I had quite a lot of fun with these plays, and the children enjoyed performing them. I began writing sketches for the Bible School children and, later on, after joining the Christian Caravan and Campers Fellowship (having bought a caravan), I became involved in the youth work of that movement, writing sketches and poems, organising meetings and activities for about two hundred teenagers. I hope my involvement has been instrumental in leading some to Christ as we always gave the children a message which had to do with the Love of Jesus. I enjoyed it all so much and, the way the young folk responded, I'm sure they did too.

The youth leader, another member of our church, invited me to work with them to stage a musical with the children, to perform at the Christian Resources Exhibition in London as well as the Luton Technical College (As it was known then). I would always help her with any musicals she staged with the adults in the church. Now I found myself working with teenagers in Bible school, and taking midweek Bible studies alongside them. How different my life had become.

When I had tried to work with teenagers in my old church, I was told there were no specialists in the assembly and was discouraged from doing anything. Now, within a short while, I was doing the very thing I loved most; being involved with the young people. I daresay my old church would be horrified with all this, and I would often think of our two children we had left behind and what their response would be. I'm sure it would be: "Mum, you've gone downhill since you left the church.

Going back to my early days with the Campaigners and my refusal to wear the uniform, I must add that Joyce did not particularly like taking the girls to the Campaigners camps each year. But, if you remember, it was at just such a Christian camp that I first came to know the Lord, so to me it was very important that these girls went to camp which meant my hang ups about uniform, had to go. "Was God so interested in what I wore? Were their souls not more important than uniforms?" If taking them to camp meant I had to go into uniform then I would go into uniform.

I began to see that so many things I had regarded as important meant nothing to God. God is interested in young people, so I took the girls to camp and continued to do so for the next thirteen years. I saw many young people respond to Christ that first year, it was a confirmation that I had done the right thing.

It was at this first camp, seeing the young people respond to the gospel, that made me think of my own young people back in my old church, who had never witnessed anything like this and were bound up by rules and regulations. Moreover, it was me who had encouraged them, all their lives I assured them that the teachings in my old church were the only ones that were right. I had been responsible for their spiritual upbringing and I was therefore responsible for where they were now, bound with religious laws.

I went up to my room because I became quite emotional and burst into tears. One of the leaders came in and wanted to know what had upset me. I explained a little of what it was and she suggested I went for prayer with the chaplain. At first I refused, I was not yet used to people praying for me, I think I was embarrassed too, but she held my hand and took me to the chaplain's wife, who said she and husband would love to pray with me.

But that evening there were so many children coming to see the chaplain, having been touched by the gospel, that it was about one o'clock in the morning before he had a chance to pray with me. I explained a little of my experiences. I still did not want to be in this position of being prayed for, but I had to accept that, now I was here, I would just have to go through with it. The chaplain and his wife put their hands on my shoulders as I shut my eyes, he said."I want you to imagine you are all bound up like a mummy and the Lord comes along and is unwinding the bandages, releasing you."

He then prayed that I would be delivered from the bonds that bound me. Then he asked me what I could see, I said, "Nothing..."

He continued praying, then again he would ask me what I could see and it was still nothing, then, like a flash I saw the Lord with His hands outstretched towards me saying:"I love you"

Then it hit me like a bolt: "If Jesus loves me, nothing else in this world matters." I am free. It was as if a veil had been lifted and all my continual striving to understand and sort out all I had been taught in my previous church and how it all fitted in to what I was seeing and learning now and trying to discover who was right and who was wrong, the continual turmoil and weariness of all that was forever going round and round in my head along with all the guilt I felt could all stop because Jesus loves me. Really, that was all I ever needed to know.

I return to that moment again and again when feelings of guilt arise and say to myself:" It doesn't matter because Jesus loves me anyway!"

John always said he did not have the same feelings of guilt that I had this maybe because the decision to leave my old church was made for him, when they threw him out, but because I had to make that decision for myself, the responsibility of what happened to our family lay on my shoulders.

We had not left our old church for long before we tried to find my brother Reg. We went through all sorts of channels to trace him but to no avail. As a last resort, we asked the Salvation Army to help us but after several weeks, they told us they had been unsuccessful. We were really disappointed, not knowing who else to turn too. Then we remembered that, at one time, Reg.worked for a shoe factory, transporting their shoes to the wholesalers, but had no idea the name of the company or, if after ten years, he would still be working for them. So we decided to phone every shoe factory in Leicester to see if we could trace him. We suffered disappointment after disappointment until, eventually, we couldn't believe it, the person at the other end of the phone said, "Yes, we know Reg.." Reg was out for the night making deliveries but he (the man on the phone) would get him to phone us when he got back. We couldn't wait!!When we told him we had left his old church, he said he felt like jumping for joy, he had thought, at first, we had phoned to say something had happened to Mother. So now I have both Reg. and Barbara back!

Moving on

I have moved on now and, thanks to the care and love we experience in the church, we have learnt what true Christianity is and what God is really looking for in our lives. He is looking for us to be like Jesus who said, "Follow me..." His actions throughout the Gospels show how He reached out to the poor and needy, how He touched the lepers, ate with sinners, healed the sick, comforted the widow, spent time with the woman at the well, and many more examples of how we should act towards one another. He never separated himself from sinners but reached out to them; dying on the cross to save them.

I am interested by what Paul says in 1 Corinthians 9: "I have become all things to all men so that by all possible means, I might save some. I do all this for the sake of the gospel that I may share in its blessings."

In verse 15, Paul goes on to say, "Though I am free and belong to no man, I made myself a slave to everyone, to win as many as possible. To the Jews, I became like a Jew to win the Jews, to those under the law, I became like one under the law, though I myself was not under the law, so as to win those under the law, to the weak, I became weak to win the weak."

Like Jesus, Paul got down to where people were. How, I ask, could he have done that if he had kept as separate as my church wanted me to do? Remember Jesus said, "Follow me..." In other words, follow my example, for this is the way to please God.

Another quote from Paul in 1 Corinthians; this time in chapter 10, comes under the heading The Believers Freedom:"Eat everything sold in the market without raising questions of conscience, for, the Earth is the Lord's and everything in it".

Then in verse 27: "If some believer invites you to a meal and you want to go, eat whatever is put before you without raising questions of conscience." I notice that

Paul is not saying there that we should not eat with unbelievers but, if any unbeliever asked you for a meal and you decide to go, that's up to you. It seems that the doctrine we were taught, in not eating with those they do not fellowship with, goes beyond Paul's ministry.

Another Scripture that has greatly helped me, this time from Acts 2:2-9

So when Peter went up to Jerusalem, the circumcised believers criticized him

and said, "You went into the house of uncircumcised men and ate with them."

Starting from the beginning, Peter told them the whole story:

"I was in the city of Joppa praying, and in a trance I saw a vision. I saw something like a large sheet being let down from heaven by its four corners, and it came down to where I was.

I looked into it and saw four-footed animals of the earth, wild beasts, reptiles and birds. Then I heard a voice telling me, 'Get up, Peter. Kill and eat.'

"I replied, 'Surely not, Lord! Nothing impure or unclean has ever entered my mouth.'

"The voice spoke from heaven a second time, 'Do not call anything impure that God has made clean.'

This happened three times, and then it was all pulled up to heaven again.

My old church would call other Christians "unclean" if they (the other Christians) did not teach their doctrines or fellowship with them, but this passage in Acts tells us not to call unclean or impure that which God has made clean.

Once, we were all common and unclean until God cleansed us, so what right do I have to dissociate or call unclean, those who have been washed in the blood of Jesus?

I rejoice now after so many years of bondage, to have come under the freedom that Christ gives. I am no longer bound by man's rules and regulations, my freedom comes in knowing that Christ loves me, and it is this that makes me a willing servant. I am no longer one that serves under bondage, but serves from the heart.

Our two children we left behind both married within the Fellowship. John and I were never told when or who they had married but found out by going to the registrar's office and, feeling most embarrassed at having to explain to them that although it might sound odd, we were looking to see if our two children had married and who they had married. To our surprise, the registrar said she knew the sect we had belonged to saying "I have a friend that left the sect and know all about them," she then suggested we come back the next day.

The following day she gave us a desk to sit at and handed us the registry books to look through, telling us to take as long as we liked. We found both their names and the partners they had married. We knew them both.

We understand our daughter now has six children and our son has five. Eleven grandchildren we have never known.

Several years later we were told that my mother had a stroke and had been taken into a nursing home in Leicester. When I heard this, I asked if I could go and see her I was refused they said they would let me know, but later told me she did not want to see me. I don't know whether this message really came from my mother or from the church in Leicester.

She evidently died some time later. We were just told that she was dead and had already been buried.

We went to Leicester to try to find her grave, my brother, Reg, who had lived in Leicester since he had left the church ten years earlier, knew most of the cemeteries in the area so he approached each cemetery asking if they had any records of my mother being buried there. Eventually we found her grave tended it and put flowers on it but it is so sad that I never got to see her again after that day I left to go back to John.

Andrew has two children, Christy and Luke and our son Luke has two girls, Diane and Ruth. At the time of writing, we have four grandchildren we love and cherish but we are so sad that we have not been able to have any contact with the eleven grandchildren that Sarah and Peter have between them.

Beth married Roy O'Hara in 2008 but, as yet, has no children. John and I are both retired now although we still carry the pain of the divisions that remain in our family, yet, we never stop praying that, one day, the Lord will reunite us all again. Whatever happens, we know that we are loved by the maker of the universe and He is not the hard and legalistic God we once thought Him to be. He is awesome, holy, righteous, and above all a God of love.

My impressions of God are encompassed in the following poem I wrote:

FREE FORGIVENESS.

Oh but the Christ who died for me on Calvary,
I'd stand condemned before a righteous God.
The God who sees the God who is all knowing,
Has marked my ways and seen the paths I've trod.
A God so great beyond my apprehension
A Holy God that cannot look on sin,
Bent down so low and offered free forgiveness,
His love, such love, through Christ my sinful heart to win.

There'll be a day when God will stand in judgement,
And but for Christ, His wrath would fall on me.
For I have heard His anger in the thunder,
And power as in the mighty roaring sea,
His governmental hand one day will deal with sin,
And yet that God supreme in Majesty,
Bent down so low and offered free for forgiveness,
His love, such love, He has through Christ bestowed on me.

Oh but for Christ when God goes forth in judgement,
Where would I stand? I tremble as I see,
My never dying soul its destination,
Would be to spend in Hell's eternity.
Banished from God the judge of all the earth and sky,
But yet this mighty God enthroned on high,
Bent down so low and offered free forgiveness,
And I shall never understand the reason why.

EPILOGUE

Since writing "My Journey to Freedom", our faith has been put to the test on several occasions but I think I have learnt that God is not, as I once thought, "Hard and legal", but is a God of love and compassion. He draws us closer to Himself through our pain and grief and, through every storm of life, He walks along side us.

When our daughter Beth's husband, Roy, died in his sleep, he left behind his children, Bradley, who was two and four month old Callum who has Down's syndrome.

I wrote the following poem because, although we felt the sorrow and pain of it, yet alongside that, we understood it was in God's planning. Nothing happens to His people by chance, there is always a reason, and in accepting His will, we find we can sing His praises through every storm.

> Your ways are not my ways, help me understand,
> For I am not yet in tune with the things you have planned,
> Why take to yourself a father of two,
> And leave a young widow dependent on you?
> A five month old child and a small boy of three?
> Your ways are not my ways Lord help me to see.
>
> Your wisdom and greatness are far beyond me,
> I know I must trust you although I can't see,
> In sorrow and sadness, in darkness of death,
> When hearts that are breaking and tears take our breath,
> Your ways are not our ways, help me understand,
> How there is wisdom and love in the things you have planned.
>
> When trees of the fields shed their leaves and lay bare,
> Lifeless, forlorn in the cold winter's air,
> Yet burst into life by the power of your hand,
> Majestically feeding and shielding the land,
> Though bare is my heart on these cold winter days,
> May it break forth in spring to your worship and praise,
>
> May we rest in your love through these days of despair,
> Awaiting the time when the fruit will be there,
> When cold winds are biting, the ground hard and bare,
> Be patient in knowing you'll always be there,

Like sun melts the frost in the days of the spring,
May we burst from the darkness your praises to sing.

And, when two years later Andrew's son (Luke) our grandson who in a deep depression died on a railway line, I wrote the following:

Who is this man who walks upon the waters?
And bids the waves and billows to be still,
Who by his will creates a vast expansion,
Of sun, moon and stars all subject to his will,
It is the Lord, who understands earth's sorrows,
The Lord who wept when Lazarus had died,
Is with us now and understands earth's sadness,
Who feels with us and stores the tears we've cried.

Who is this man God likened to a shepherd?
Who searches night and day for one lost sheep?
One child, one son lost in life's stream of madness,
One boy who slipped and could not find his feet,
But Jesus found and placed him on his shoulders,
He found him there upon a railway track,
And took him home, home to himself of rejoicing,
From earth to heaven to claim his loved one back.

Who is this man who gave himself for sinners?
And took upon himself the debt we owe?
So that those who look to Him may be forgiven,
They ask not who he is because they know,
Our hearts respond in love beyond our sorrow,
Rejoice in him who feels our every pain,
We have a hope; we have a bright tomorrow,
With Christ and when our loved ones meet again.

Christ broke the chains of sin and death that bind us,
And those that trust in him will see his face,
Will live forever in the Saviour's presence,
Made perfect through Christ's death, what love, what grace,
To be forever living in his presence,
All earth's painful sorrows turned to bliss,
Rejoicing in a land of milk and honey,
His faithful one's absorbing all of this.

www.ingramcontent.com/pod-product-compliance
Lightning Source LLC
Chambersburg PA
CBHW070953080526
44587CB00015B/2293